THE

IMPROVEMENT

ENGINE

THE

IMPROVEMENT

ENGINE

Creativity & Innovation
Through Employee Involvement

EDITED BY
THE
JAPAN HUMAN RELATIONS ASSOCIATION

◆

FOREWORD BY
STEPHEN J. ANSUINI

◆

PUBLISHER'S MESSAGE BY
NORMAN BODEK

the kaizen teian system

PRODUCTIVITY PRESS

PORTLAND, OREGON

Originally published as Kaizen Teian III by Nikkan Kogyo Shimbun, Ltd., Tokyo.
© 1990 Nikkan Kogyo Shimbun, Ltd.

Edited by the Japan Human Relations Association
Text of Parts 1,2 & 3 by Bunji Tozawa, Managing Editor, JHRA
Illustrations and cartoons by Kiyonori Kuriko, Akiko Yamamoto, and Misako Fukui

English edition © 1995 Productivity Press, Inc. Translated by Steve and Yumi Johnson.

Productivity Press
P.O. Box 13390
Portland, OR 97213-0390
United States of America
Telephone: 503-235-0600
Telefax: 503-235-0909

Design and composition by Rohani Design, Edmonds, Washington
Printed and bound by Edward Brothers in the United States of America

04 03 02 01 00 99 98 97 96 95   9 8 7 6 5 4 3 2 1

Library of Congress Cataloging-in-Publication Data:
Kaizen teian III. English
    The improvement engine : creativity and innovation through employee involvement : the kaizen teian system / edited by the Japan Human Relations Association : foreword by Stephen J. Ansuini : publisher's message by Norman Bodek : [translated by Steve and Yumi Johnson]. -- English ed.
       p. cm.
    Translation of: Kaizen teian III.
    Includes index.
    ISBN: 1-56327-010-2
    1. Suggestion systems--Japan.   2. Problem solving.   3. Creative ability in business--Japan.   4. Industrial management--Japan--Employee participation.   5. Industrial efficiency--Japan.
    I. Nihon HR Kyōkai. II. Title.
HF5549.5.S8K3515 1995
658.3'14--dc20   94-45511
                                                           CIP

CONTENTS

PART TWO
How to Use the Kaizen Sheet as a Tool

PART FOUR
Kaizen Teian Examples

Show me a company that's uninterested in continuous improvement, and I'll show you a company that may not be in business by the beginning of the twenty-first century. Competition for key global markets is steadily increasing. Companies that want to keep current customers while acquiring new ones must seize new opportunities while efficiently adapting to changing markets.

Companies in Japan have come to realize that shifting people's perceptions about improvement activities makes a big difference. As *The Improvement Engine* points out, if managers and supervisors take the right approach, people feel more confident about reporting what they've already accomplished. Earlier in the evolution of improvement proposal systems, companies often placed great pressure on their people to write and submit improvements. When faced with blank improvement forms, employees would feel that only superlative ideas should be submitted. This was somewhat intimidating, and it was probably one of the key reasons why participation reached respectable levels instead of very high levels. With the shift in understanding accompanying the development of kaizen reporting, however, participation levels soared, thus so did the flow of truly useful improvement ideas.

The *kaizen reporting system,* the subject of this book, is a powerful tool for "uncovering" unconscious improvements and developing the skills used to detect problems, solve problems, and implement improvements. The goal is to make improvement a conscious habit rather than an occasional event. It is human nature to make improvements, and often we do so unconsciously. You can begin to understand how if you take a moment to recall some small improvement you've made recently at home. Perhaps you drilled holes in the handles of several yard tools so that you could hang them from your garage wall.

Were you aware of what you were doing when you implemented such a small improvement? Or did you implement it without giving it much thought? The same phenomenon occurs in the workplace. In the workplace, however, small improvements may contribute to increased productivity and better quality. Thus the financial incentive for making improvement a habit rather than an occasional occurrence is obvious. Yet how often do companies establish goals to create a culture of continuous improvement? Moreover, how does a company seeking to create such a culture ensure that daily work activities address this crucial value? The kaizen reporting system provides the best means of doing so, and *The Improvement Engine* presents the most refined thinking available to date regarding employee improvement systems.

Part One of *The Improvement Engine* outlines the foundation for continuous improvement within your company. In this section you'll learn

- how and why continuous improvement proposal systems evolved from traditional suggestion systems
- how to use the kaizen sheet as an effective tool for better continuous improvement and human resources development; plus, how to use a suggestion system effectively
- tips for activating and maintaining a vital kaizen reporting system
- simple evaluation standards for both first-stage and upper-grade improvements

Part Two explains how the kaizen sheet can effectively teach people the improvement process. In addition, this section also demonstrates how to

- ease anxieties about the documentation of improvements
- "prime the improvement pump"
- use the kaizen sheet to understand problems clearly
- use the kaizen sheet for evaluations that focus on employees' strengths

Part Three focuses on the ways in which practical examples of simple workplace improvements drive kaizen activities. In addition to providing replicas of some examples that have worked well for other companies and telling you how to make the best use of examples generated by your own employees, this section clarifies a few other important points:

- why the horizontal deployment of ideas does not work
- how kaizen relates to innovation and small group activities—including a discussion of how to safeguard against superficial improvements
- the importance of promotional materials that focus on small workplace improvements

Part Four illustrates in case studies the principles discussed in Parts One through Three. Six narratives cover a spectrum of ideas from simple to complex. Yuko Ishida of Fujicolor Services tells about creating a miniature directory for a fax machine. This is a good example of a first-stage improvement. Chikara Kairiku of Osaka Natural Gas, on the other hand, reports the development of a sophisticated wear sensor for a BOG compressor—an upper-grade improvement to be sure! Whether the examples are simple or sophisticated, each is the result of careful thought. The person who's implemented the improvement has taken great care—often overcoming many frustrations—to create counter-measures that adequately address root causes.

Bunji Tozawa, managing editor with the Japan Human Relations Association (JHRA) and a world-class expert on kaizen teian systems, developed much of the material in the Kaizen Teian series, which includes the two volumes that preceded *The Improvement Engine: Kaizen Teian 1* and *Kaizen Teian 2*. He also compiled the material that many of you know as *The Idea Book* (Productivity Press, 1988). Mr. Tozawa's tireless work has transformed the the continuous improvement proposal system into the management process described in this book. In addition to writing and editing JHRA's monthly magazine, *Ingenuity and Inventions*, Mr. Tozawa also lectures and presents workshops in the United States, Europe, and Japan. We greatly appreciate his assistance and that of Kenjiro Yamada, managing director of JHRA, in bringing about this translation.

Our special thanks to Miho Matsubara for assistance in clarifying the translation. A number of other people helped make this book possible: Bill Stanton, production manager; Diane Asay, acquisitions editor; Karen Jones, managing editor; Barry Shulak, development editor; Susan Swanson, production coordinator; and Rohani Design, book design and composition.

Norman Bodek
Publisher

The *Improvement Engine* contains lots of practical advice for developing a workforce that "lives" continuous improvement. Developing such a workforce, of course, depends upon the commitment of management at all levels. In other words, we must "walk the talk" before our employees will listen to us. It's a step back to basics. At Toyota Motor Manufacturing, U.S.A. (TMM), we've been emphasizing the basics since day one. As a result, we have a workforce that's enthusiastic about continuous improvement.

When we receive visitors at our plant, which is located in Georgetown, Kentucky, they frequently behave as if we're holding out—as if we have some "magic wand" that we won't allow them to see. Obviously there is no magic wand. Yet the image persists. Why? In a word, "kaizen." Kaizen is the Japanese word for a companywide approach to continuous improvement. Kaizen is a key to competitive success in today's world market; it's the "improvement engine" to which the title of this book refers. I believe that any organization without an improvement engine of some type will quickly be overtaken by its competition. In addition, it's imperative that this improvement engine, in whatever form it takes, be as simple as possible. All too often management tends to overcomplicate systems.

Time and again I'm amazed by individuals, both in management and on the shop floor, who feel compelled to make things as convoluted as possible. Throw technology into the mix and you compound the problem. Technological "solutions" are usually expensive and often not even necessary. Frankly, I think people come up with such solutions because of a need to show that they are educated and skilled. And then there are those people who possess so much business savvy, it simply never occurs to them that simple may be better.

So here we are again—back to the basics. I am not suggesting that kaizen activities are simple. Nor am I saying that it is always inappropriate to make use of technology to implement improvements. I only mean to say that you need to aim for the following targets: a simple administrative structure and only truly appropriate uses of technology.

This is easier said than done. At TMM, for example, a group of seven team members wanted to reduce an inconvenience in the part of our plant in which vehicle bodies are painted and sealed. This particular group is responsible for waterproofing seams in the engine compartment and trunk of each car. In the course of their work, they use jigs similar to the rods that hold the hood open on a finished car. They use these jigs repeatedly, as do other teams within this part of the plant. Before the improvement, after using a jig they would toss it into a container which weighed about 50 to 70 pounds, and they would have to carry this thing to another part of the floor.

After almost four months of wrestling with this problem, they proposed a countermeasure that employed a conveyor system. It would have cost over $250,000 to make this improvement. Their manager agreed that something needed to be done, but—and this probably comes as no surprise—he said that their solution was too expensive to implement. He asked them to devise another solution that would cost less. One month later, the team returned with a less complicated countermeasure. This solution relied upon a semi-powered system that delivered the jig to a certain height, after which it slid along a rail to the next site where it was needed. This system would have cost a mere $40,000.

At this point, most of us would have said, "Great job. Let's do it." But their manager said that although the latest proposal was a significant improvement over the first, the cost was still too high. Again, he asked them to find another solution. Three weeks later, after not merely looking, but actually *seeing* what they were looking at, the team returned with a back-to-basics countermeasure that cost absolutely nothing. In this area of the plant, two lines move parallel to one another in opposite directions. At this stage in the manufacturing process, you're dealing just with a unibody frame. The bumpers haven't been attached yet. Therein lay the solution to the team's problem: They realized they could store a jig within the tubular section of the unibody frame to which the rear bumper attaches. To minimize movement, they could retrieve a jig from the rear of the unibody frame in the adjacent line. Coming up with this elegantly simple improvement was an eye-opening experience for them. It's changed the way they approach new challenges.

The Improvement Engine can help you change the way you approach the challenge of sustaining a vital continuous improvement system. This book beautifully illustrates the concept that simple is better. As it points out, a simple administrative structure combined with training and promotional materials that emphasize simple examples will help you start and sustain your own improvement engine. Keep in mind that the speed with which workers embrace improvement activities depends not only upon management's support, but also upon the way management responds to successes and failures. Again, it's really important to "walk the talk." In effect, managers communicate their company's philosophy through their behavior—i.e., through the activities they support and the ways they handle their administrative responsibilities. Here are some of the key "behavioral" elements identified in *The Improvement Engine* that directly correlate to our philosophy at TMM:

- visible management support
- simple administration
- clear focus on the immediate work area (having employees document improvements they have already made)
- continuous emphasis on employee participation
- daily recognition of employee efforts
- use of a strong developmental and evaluative tool

The Improvement Engine will be useful to managers, supervisors, and administrators regardless of their experience with continuous improvement systems. However, I would strongly recommend that you read it not just to learn or review the mechanics of kaizen systems, but to understand the many implications of the concepts and principles the book presents. For me, one of the most thought-provoking sections of this book is the first part, "Simple System, Elaborate Benefits." Ponder this title after reading this section and you will be amazed at the many subtleties these few words convey.

If you are just beginning to activate a continuous improvement system in your plant, allow me to point out three ideas contained in this book that will be crucial to your success:

1. Pay attention to what people are doing right, and make sure you praise them for it.
2. Don't expect everyone to hit a home run. In other words, emphasize small improvements.
3. Be sure to have people document conditions both before and after improvements. Otherwise, it will be difficult to determine the benefits.

In closing, I urge you again to think carefully about the information in this book. Open yourself to a paradigm shift so that you're not just going through the motions of running a continuous improvement system, but embracing it as a truly life-changing experience.

Stephen J. Ansuini
Employee Education and Training Specialist
Toyota Motor Manufacturing, U.S.A., Inc.

At the Japan Human Relations Association we field lots of questions about kaizen teian systems. In particular, companies frequently ask us what they can do to activate a system, and whether we have any remedies for improvement activities that have become stagnant. The implied question that nobody asks is: Do we really have to jump through all kinds of hoops to activate and promote a kaizen teian system?

Absolutely not. In fact, you should purge the system of all complications that result in cumbersome rules and management systems. Such things will only confuse people and dampen their enthusiasm for kaizen activities. Simplify things, however, and you're sure to see high participation levels.

This book highlights three concerns:

1. Clarifying the difference between kaizen and suggestions
2. Using the kaizen sheet as a tool
3. Using practical examples to drive kaizen activities

A good understanding of these three things is all the formal knowledge that's needed to successfully activate a kaizen system. No other "how to" materials are needed. It's possible to get lots of promotional ideas and know-how from books. But if you hope to activate and promote kaizen activities in spite of time, staffing and budget constraints, you're better off simply forging ahead. As long as you have your priorities straight, you'll be able to learn as you go. In the beginning, it's enough that you understand

- what you should do
- what you must do
- what is best to do

This book illuminates these three points and will also help you keep things simple and on track.

Overzealous promoters often tend to set up complex regulations, collect overly detailed data, and compile books full of impressive examples. Unfortunately, such books are practically useless; no one will read them. This book shows you how simple examples and simple management ensure the activation of a vital kaizen system.

When you get to the core of a problem, you can't help but simplify it, and thereby achieve significant improvements. The purpose of improvement activities is to make work more efficient, but the prerequisite for workplace efficiency is a simple, competently managed kaizen system.

For the sake of consistency, conversion to dollars from yen in this book is based on the exchange rate of .007 (142.86 yen per U.S. dollar). This is an average rate chosen by the translators to reflect fluctuating rates during 1990, the year the Japanese language version was published.

The actual figures are, in a way, irrelevant. The important thing to remember is that a continuous improvement proposal system like the one introduced in this book emphasizes small workplace improvements and thus small rewards. In fact, according to data supplied by the JHRA (see the introductory comments for Chapter 14), and accounting for fluctuating exchange rates, it's fairly safe to say that 90 to 95 percent of all participants in kaizen teian systems in Japan earn rewards of about five dollars or less.

PART

ONE

SIMPLE SYSTEM, ELABORATE BENEFIT

The secret of a successful kaizen teian activation is not to do lots of jobs, but to stop doing the complicated and unnecessary ones. By clarifying the difference between a kaizen teian system and a traditional suggestion system, we will show you why a kaizen teian system provides a simpler and more effective means of ensuring your continued success.

WHEN ABOLISHING A TRADITIONAL SUGGESTION SYSTEM IS THE BEST THING TO DO

How often have you heard the following comments in your workplace?

- "This is unnecessary work."
- "Why are we doing this when we are so busy?"
- "It's a real burden."
- "This is slowing me down."

It is all too common to hear such comments among workers in companies where traditional suggestion activities are promoted. In such instances you should immediately terminate the suggestion system in use. Although this may seem a radical action, it will pave the way for the small, simple, incremental improvements that are the lifeblood of kaizen teian (continuous improvement through implemented proposals).

EMPLOY AN IMPROVEMENT PROPOSAL SYSTEM THAT PROMOTES SIMPLICITY AND CLARITY

The main principles of kaizen are:

- stop doing whatever is trivial
- stop doing whatever is wasteful
- stop doing whatever is unnecessary

Initially, traditional suggestion systems were introduced with work efficiency as one of the main objectives. Yet if people are making comments like those above, then the system itself is the primary obstacle to the objective. If this is true, isn't it better to eliminate the suggestion system? Work is sure to improve considerably. And this is a step in the right direction.

Companies that are serious about continuous improvement have found that improvement proposal systems are superior to traditional suggestion systems. In such companies, you might hear "This system is really useful for improving work efficiency," or "It's a perfect system. It gives us the opportunity to promote personal and professional growth."

What accounts for such different results? It's the fundamental difference between kaizen teian, and its emphasis on small, incremental improvements, and traditional suggestion systems, which, in effect, discourage such improvements. Managed properly, a kaizen teian system is a powerful tool for success.

SIMPLICITY AND CLARITY ARE THE KEYS TO SUCCESS

Companies that are not good at handling suggestion systems usually misunderstand some important concepts:

- the difference between kaizen and suggestions
- the relationship between kaizen and innovation

4

- the relationship between the work of one's own department and other departments

Traditional suggestion systems lump all these different things together. A kaizen teian system, on the other hand, clarifies such differences, relationships, and the focus of improvement activities. This results in a more pleasant and orderly workplace.

Companies that have achieved great results promoting continuous improvement activities have the following three things in common:

1. a clear understanding of the concept of continuous improvement through implemented proposals
2. a precise main objective
3. a system and corresponding rules that are simple

If a company keeps these things in mind while organizing and maintaining kaizen teian activities, it too is bound to be successful.

THE FOUR AREAS IN WHICH IMPROVEMENT ACTIVITIES TAKE PLACE

As you can see from the diagram on page 6, small improvements in one's own work area comprise just one of four components of a system in which general knowledge, ideas, and information from all employees get filtered up to management.

Continuous Improvement Proposal Systems Focus on the Immediate Work Area

As the diagram also shows, in terms of job responsibility, work can be separated into one's own job and other people's jobs. Doesn't it make sense that people can improve things best in the area they know best? With the guidance and approval of

5

The Four Areas in which Kaizen Activities Take Place

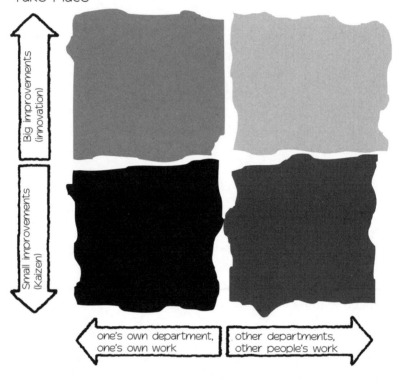

Big Improvements (innovation)

Small Improvements (Kaizen)

one's own department, one's own work

other departments, other people's work

a supervisor, employees can implement proposals that greatly improve their own work and the work of their departments. In fact, progressive companies understand that job descriptions are flexible in the sense that employees may use their creativity and discretion to make such improvements. Job descriptions may clearly define the *extent* of an employee's discretion, but they need not interfere with his or her inclination to devise creative solutions to problems. In many Japanese companies, there is quite a wide "gray area," in that there are workplaces in which, regardless of rules and regulations, the willingness and ability of an employee will eventually determine his or her job duties and responsibilities.

If employees are aware of problems in their own area of responsibility they can improve them through their own initiative. However, when something exceeds their authority, they need the support and cooperation of a supervisor. In other words, once a person has secured the backing and encouragement of his or her supervisor, there need be no limit to the extent of the improvement one may implement.

The scope of other people's work, however, is the area into which individual workers cannot go as far. One cannot make any improvements without consulting the department concerned. This is the domain of the traditional suggestion system, in which improvements ideas take the form of suggestions, requests, and demands. Improvement ideas don't become improvements until they are implemented. To involve another department often decreases the chances that one will see his or her idea implemented.

This isn't always true, though. If someone's supervisor, for instance, is responsible for the department in which the idea originated and for the department to which the idea is addressed, then it is not uncommon for the boundaries between the two departments to blur—especially if the work of one department "feeds" the work of the next. But this is the exception to the general rule that continuous improvement proposals are best confined to one's immediate work area.

INNOVATION AND KAIZEN: TWO WAYS TO SMASH THE STATUS QUO

Look again at the diagram on page 6. We've already discussed the horizontal aspect of the diagram—the difference between one's own work and other people's work. Now we turn to a discussion of the diagram's vertical aspect, in which kaizen signifies improvements made as a result of ongoing efforts to break through the status quo. Innovations, on the other hand, according to Masaaki Imai, "involve dramatic alterations to the status quo as a result of large investments in new technology or equipment."* While the emphasis in innovation is on the benefits derived from significant investment and special skills, the emphasis in kaizen is on the achievement of small break-throughs by normal employees using common sense and ingenuity to change the way they do their daily work.

In their own work areas people can energetically pursue improvement activities and submit kaizen reports (more on this in Part Two). If improvement ideas relate to someone else's work, one can pass along ideas and information to that department in the form of suggestions.

Innovation, however, since it involves a large amount of investment (risk) and specialized skills, lies within the domain of managers, engineers, and other specialists. "Normal" employees can still make suggestions—in effect, provide ideas and informa-tion—that may contribute to innovation. But they must realize that the form their ideas take will be shaped by other people.

THE ROLE OF INDIVIDUALS IN KAIZEN AND INNOVATION

Another way of looking at the diagram on page 6 is as a rep-resentation of the four ways of changing present conditions:

A. continuous improvement of one's own work
B. continuous improvement of other people's work
C. innovation within one's own department
D. innovation within other departments

In traditional suggestion systems, as we mentioned earlier, these four areas have been jumbled together, and this has resulted

---

*Masaaki Imai, *Kaizen: The Key to Japan's Competitive Success* (New York: McGraw-Hill; 1986), p.6

The Four Ways of Changing the Status Quo

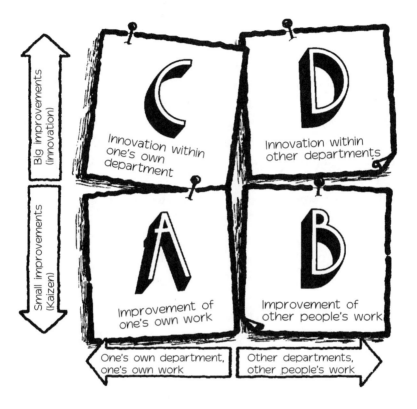

in confusion and misunderstanding. The development of the kaizen reporting system, which we will discuss in more depth in the next chapter, does much to eliminate confusion and efficiently channel information and ideas relevant to the four areas we've identified.

Area A, of course, is the one we're most concerned about in this book. Great things happen when a company promotes continuous improvement activities by setting up a kaizen reporting system. In areas B, C, and D, the best approach is to facilitate the flow of information within the company with the help of a suggestion system.

Depending upon the level of a company's commitment to continuous improvement, area B may also be a fertile area for implementing ideas that originated in area A. A company establishes a system that recognizes the worth of good ideas, then it doesn't matter ultimately where the idea came from. It's the implemented improvement that counts.

On the other hand, innovation in areas C and D is elaborate, and cannot easily be tackled on a routine basis. When companies want to solicit ideas from non-specialists, they often find it helpful to establish themes and finite time periods for specific suggestion activities. Combined with a simple structure for evaluating suggestions, this approach ensures that employees may contribute to innovations in areas C and D.

Otherwise, some very good ideas will probably go to waste. Should this be the case, not only will ideas be wasted, but employees will become distrustful of management.

KAIZEN TEIAN STRETCHES PERSONAL AND COMPANY BOUNDARIES

The boundaries of areas A, B, C, and D vary according to the willingness, ability, and position of the individual. Since the president of a company is responsible for the entire operation, all areas of his or her work in effect can be classified as belonging to area A. He or she has the authority and power to execute plans and implement improvements that cannot be handled by others.

Similarly, others within the corporate hierarchy have "A" areas commensurate with the extent of their responsibility. The point here, as we alluded to earlier, is that the area defined as "one's own work" is flexible. By participating in kaizen activities, employees develop the skills and abilities that enlarge

- the scope of individual responsibility
- the extent of daily control over the work

Employee's Role in a Company that Restricts Kaizen Activities

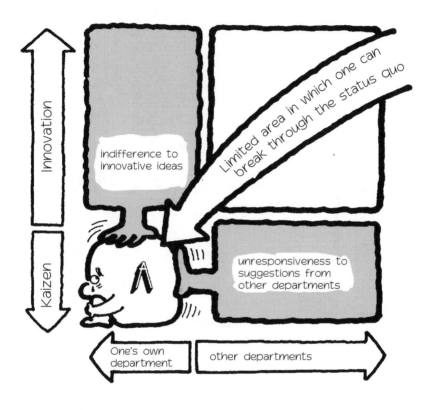

To enlarge the area of one's own work is to increase a person's value as an employee.

Which type of company will be stronger, then? One that restricts its employees' improvement activities or one that encourages them? The latter type achieves fairly important breakthroughs on a daily basis, the former type fosters indecision and maintains the status quo. Such a company never takes initiatives or breaks new ground; it simply follows in its competitors' footsteps.

Employee's Role in a Company that Encourages Kaizen Activities

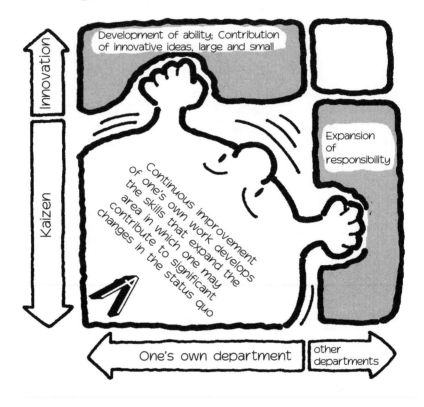

12

In companies where everyone tries to stretch their personal (area A) boundaries (although they might appear to be encroaching on other people's turf), the company's overall boundaries continue to widen. Conversely, in companies where the boundaries are narrow, there is a tendency to concede problems rather than try to solve them. In a company like this it is common to hear such comments as, "That's outside my realm of responsibility," and, "I don't have the ability to deal with that," and "I'll have to put it forward at the next meeting." A loser's climate seems to have been created.

Of course, a company's success depends upon many factors: the economic climate, market forces, products, sales and financial ability, and so on. Yet consider the possibilities for overall corporate health if a company actively engages the creative potential of all its employees. By providing a mechanism that gives employees an opportunity to stretch their individual boundaries, a company subsequently expands corporate boundaries, influencing its destiny in a most positive way.

We believe that a company's success depends greatly on the emphasis its management places upon bottom-up activities such as kaizen teian. Does your company promote a system for continuous improvement that expands employees' boundaries? Does it contribute to corporate success by shattering the status quo? Or does it maintain the status quo?

Tapping Human Resources Through Use of Venture Systems

Many people are quite amazing in their capacity to generate unique and innovative ideas. But when they decide to or are asked to implement their ideas, the brakes come on. Suddenly they must confront such issues as responsibility, costs, precedents, and other people's opinions. People accustomed to preserving the status quo will not be able to take the next step.

People who have been developing their skills and abilities through kaizen teian activities, however, are much more likely to possess the confidence and know-how to implement their ideas. For this reason, venture systems have been adopted in many Japanese companies in order to recruit internally enterprising people who have the wherewithal to implement their ideas related to new business and product development. Of course, it is not enough for these people to possess guts and willingness; they also need proficiency in business principles. (Participation in kaizen activities also may develop such skills.)

All companies are filled to the brim with unique and innovative ideas. Throughout history, we have never run out of ideas.

What we lack are people who are able to

- recognize the value of ideas
- embrace the challenge of figuring out how to implement ideas
- assume the risks and responsibilities
- support and cooperate with others

The existence of venture systems is a logical extension of the notion that a person's job description can expand in direct proportion to his or her accumulation of skills and knowledge. Venture systems tap people rather than ideas; kaizen teian systems develop people.

Kaizen Empowers People to Make Significant Contributions in More than One Area

14

It should be clear by now why it is so important to develop people and their capacity for implementing ideas, rather than simply soliciting suggestions. Suggestions for improvement are useless unless they are implemented. This is a fundamental premise of the kaizen teian system.

In companies where suggestion activities have become a burden, small workplace improvements, large departmental improvements, improvements across departments, and improvements at the corporate level are not distinguished from one another. Small improvements, big suggestions built on dreams rather than reality, and requests and demands all get jumbled together. Then, amidst the confusion, it is common to hear urgent requests for more management support, more aggressive promotion, more workforce participation, and greater emphasis on quality. Employees at the workplace feel pressured to meet all sorts of goals and objectives. But often the goals and objectives are not really relevant to the immediate tasks at hand. Understandably, this creates a great deal of frustration.

Kaizen Empowers People to Make Significant Contributions — in More than One Area

Another common source of frustration results from what we call "suggestion games." This occurs when a company creates a complex system for evaluating people's suggestions.*

In effect, this leads to long delays in solving problems, which subsequently diminishes people's enthusiasm for improvement activities. From the employees' perspective, it feels as though management is playing games—not taking their ideas seriously.

---

*Kaizen teian systems emphasize quick, on-the-spot evaluation. Refer to chapters 6 and 7.

Quick evaluation and prompt action are priorities in a kaizen teian system, however. But more than this, kaizen activities, by developing people's work and business skills, make it possible for individuals and companies to thrive. Kaizen activities create an improvement-oriented environment in which it is possible to participate in as many as four general types of improvement:

A. implementing small workplace improvements
B. contributing to the implementation of innovative improvements in one's own department through participation in small groups
C. making informed suggestions to other departments
D. contributing to new business opportunities or new product development

In other words, a person's ability to make contributions within his or her company is theoretically unlimited. When an improvement sensibility pervades a company, people at all levels tend to be more receptive to ideas. Therefore, with the right systems in place, all kinds of good ideas may lead to implemented improvements. Kaizen is the key.

CLARIFYING THE DIFFERENCES BETWEEN TRADITIONAL SUGGESTION SYSTEMS AND THE KAIZEN TEIAN SYSTEM

Lately, the expression "implemented teian" has become popular in many Japanese companies. "Teian" means "suggestion" or "proposal," and "implemented teian" is understood as a process in which employees make improvements in the way they do their work and then submit their suggestions for doing so after the fact. When you think about it, "implemented teian" is a strange expression because it identifies as a suggestion something that is actually an improvement! That is why we prefer to use the term "kaizen reporting."

HOW KAIZEN EVOLVED FROM THE TRADITIONAL SUGGESTION SYSTEM

After World War II, Japanese industry learned a lot of management control methods from the United States, and the suggestion system was among them. The way the traditional suggestion system worked was that employees simply made suggestions, and then it was up to a designated evaluation committee to decide which ideas were to be adopted. If an employee's idea was adopted, the company paid him or her a reward.

Over the past fifty years, however, suggestion activities in Japan have evolved. What began to happen is that progressive thinkers in management saw that if companies were to cope with constantly shifting conditions in the business world, it made a great deal of sense to transfer more authority for implementation of improvements to front-line workers. The emphasis changed from *suggesting* ideas for improvement to *proposing* ideas that workers could implement themselves. The aim was continuous incremental improvement of the way of work (kaizen); the means was the development of employees through improvement proposals (teian).

The development aspect cannot be underestimated. Kaizen teian activities became, in effect, a form of on-the-job training (OJT). Participation in kaizen teian activities typically involved—and still does involve—ways of strengthening employees' skills in the following ways:

- identification of problems and improvement opportunities
- problem solving
- decision making and implementation

To summarize, the evolution from the traditional suggestion system to the continuous improvement proposal system (kaizen teian) was helped along by the fact that the latter system provided a better means of developing human resources and ability.

THE EMERGENCE OF KAIZEN REPORTING

As mentioned before, the word "teian" does mean suggestion, and this sometimes creates confusion for companies wishing to promote a kaizen teian system. This is why we prefer to think of kaizen teian as a continuous improvement proposal system. This underscores the difference between the passive nature of the traditional suggestion system and the active nature of the kaizen teian system.

To those familiar with the evolution of suggestion systems in Japan it is understood that the kaizen teian system is in fact composed of two systems: the kaizen reporting system and the suggestion system.

At some point after Japanese companies adopted the suggestion system from America, the concept of continuous improvement represented by the word "kaizen" became important; thus the phrase "kaizen teian" was created. Later, more importance was attached to continuous improvement than to suggestions, and presently this is even more true. Kaizen reporting presently represents the best means of developing the skills used for detecting problems, solving problems, and implementing improvements. In fact, the objective is to develop skills to the point that improvement becomes second nature and employees are implementing improvements and then reporting them in writing after the fact. In effect, then, the kaizen reporting system operates quite independently from any traditional suggestion system that might be in place.

Japanese companies presently attach so much importance to implemented continuous improvement ideas that conventional suggestion systems tend to be disregarded. Should this continue to happen, there is a serious concern that the suggestion system which—as we pointed out in the last chapter—still has value as a mechanism of information exchange, might disappear entirely.

When it is recognized that the kaizen teian system and the suggestion system are independent systems, however, there is no reason why they cannot coexist and even positively influence each other.

19

THE MEANS AND THE SYSTEM CHANGE
OVER TIME

The time line below shows how kaizen teian as a bottom-up movement has evolved, changed, and developed with the times, according to the needs of each era. Of course, this movement is likely to change further in response to future changes in the business environment.

Ideally, someday there would be no need for a system at all. Employees would commit themselves to keeping their companies competitive by implementing improvement ideas without expecting rewards or having to be persuaded to participate.

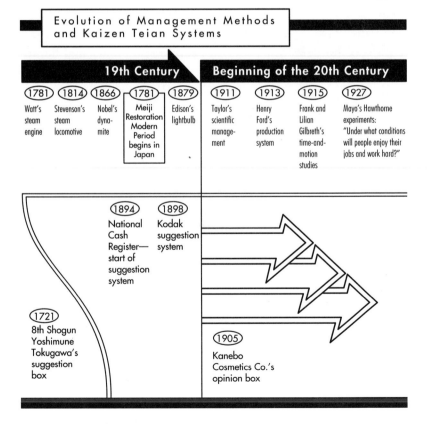

Evolution of Management Methods and Kaizen Teian Systems

19th Century

- (1781) Watt's steam engine
- (1814) Stevenson's steam locomotive
- (1866) Nobel's dynamite
- (1781) Meiji Restoration Modern Period begins in Japan
- (1879) Edison's lightbulb

Beginning of the 20th Century

- (1911) Taylor's scientific management
- (1913) Henry Ford's production system
- (1915) Frank and Lilian Gilbreth's time-and-motion studies
- (1927) Mayo's Hawthorne experiments: "Under what conditions will people enjoy their jobs and work hard?"

- (1894) National Cash Register—start of suggestion system
- (1898) Kodak suggestion system

- (1721) 8th Shogun Yoshimune Tokugawa's suggestion box

- (1905) Kanebo Cosmetics Co.'s opinion box

In order to get fractionally closer to this ideal state, it is necessary, however, that management provide a structure and develop a strategy for guiding kaizen teian efforts.

The objective of a bottom-up system is to develop the skills of employees and instill in them a strong spirit of continuous improvement. Whether you call the system you create to accomplish this a kaizen system or a suggestion system is not really important. The system is simply the means of reaching the target and the means vary greatly according to circumstances and changes in society. For this reason, the system should never become an end in itself. (For a more detailed discussion of this point, refer to Chapter 12.)

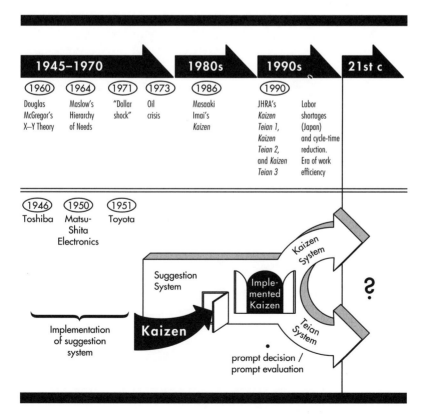

THE HUGE DIFFERENCE BETWEEN KAIZEN REPORTING AND TRADITIONAL SUGGESTION SYSTEMS

The major difference between the kaizen teian system and a suggestion system can be summarized in the following two points:

1. Kaizen reporting is implementing improvements of your own work, then submitting reports after the fact. A reward is paid.
2. With the suggestion system, you submit ideas, opinions and requests—not necessarily restricted to your own work area. In effect, no reward is paid.

KAIZEN SYSTEMS ARE BUILT FOR SPEED

With the traditional suggestion system, employees' ideas are evaluated and the small percentage of ideas that actually get implemented are rewarded. One of the drawbacks of such a system is that it consumes time, and such a leisurely approach is no longer practical. What is required in this ever-changing, competitive era, is promptness—quick decisions, judgment, and implementation—or businesses cannot survive. For this reason, the emphasis has shifted from suggestions to implemented improvement proposals. This is kaizen reporting.

Compare the rewards paid for unimplemented suggestions with those paid for implemented suggestions, and you get a clear idea of the importance attached to each. Some companies have continued to pay a reward of ¥50 ($.35) or ¥100 ($.70) for unimplemented suggestions. With the kaizen reporting system, however, the minimum reward is ¥500 (about $3.50), demonstrating the clear gap between the worth of suggestions and implemented improvement proposals.

Communicating clearly the colossal difference between kaizen and suggestions is the important thing. Unless there is a clear distinction, everything will be placed in the same basket.

INVESTMENT ACCORDING TO IMPORTANCE

The distinction between kaizen and suggestions lies not just in the reward. There is also a great difference in the way a suggestion is handled after submission. With a suggestion system, we recommend that the following regulations be clarified:

1. Individual suggestions will not be answered
2. Individuals may not claim responsibility for the implementation of an improvement or the development of a product that may have occurred as a result of a suggestion

People may say that this is too harsh. But taking such a stance allows a company to give more credit for the implementation of kaizen, and put more energy into it.

Success in corporate activities depends on how limited managerial resources (people, money, time, etc.) are doled out.

Kaizen Empowers People to Make Significant
Contributions — in More Than Just One Area

Naturally, to use resources most effectively, a company distributes them according to its priorities.

If a company presently is wasting time and energy on an ineffective suggestion system, doesn't it make better sense to devote resources to promoting kaizen implementation? We do not mean to suggest it's necessary to simply abandon suggestion systems. But it is necessary to clarify, as we did in the previous chapter, when it is appropriate to make suggestions and when it is appropriate to implement improvement proposals; because if kaizen teian activities and suggestion activities are mixed together, neither system will demonstrate its full potential. In order to make the most of kaizen and suggestions, you have to divide and regulate "the flow of traffic." See pages 26 and 27 for a list of basic rules governing the submission of suggestions and kaizen reports.

The suggestion system has value and meaning of its own. It may provide an effective mechanism for internal communication, allowing the free exchange of information and ideas across

KAIZEN Reporting Rules

1 PURPOSE

The purpose is "to make my job and the work of my department better by implementing improvements."

(1) Participation: Ingenuity and creative thinking are encouraged, and active participation is promoted.

(2) Skill development: Kaizen reporting represents an occasion for "real life on-the-job training." Communicating regularly with one's supervisor helps develop skills.

(3) Effect: The aim is to create an improvement-oriented workplace in which people perform duties easily and efficiently in a pleasant environment.

2 TARGET

(1) All employees must make improvements to their immediate work areas and write them up in Kaizen reports.

(2) Everyone from the president to the line supervisors must promote Kaizen activities. Providing guidance to others is an important job.

3 SUBMITTING KAIZEN

(1) Obtain a supervisor approval for an improvement either orally or by submitting a Kaizen consultation sheet. Ask for guidance, collaboration, or assistance as appropriate.

(2) Improve the way work is done, and whenever there is any benefit, write the improvement on the Kaizen reporting sheet and submit it to supervisors.

4 METHOD OF EVALUATION

(1) Supervisors are responsible for prompt evaluation of Kaizen sheets; they must respond to improvement proposals or consultation sheets and provide necessary guidance.

(2) Details of evaluation standards, rules, reward systems, management, and all administration are separately defined. (In order to cope with various situations, the improvement committee has authority to revise the rules at its discretion.)

3 OWNERSHIP

(1) All ownership rights relating to improvement belong to the company

(2) In case the right of industrial ownership is applied for, a separate application must be submitted in accordance with the job-related invention regulations.

Suggestion System Rules

1 PURPOSE

The purpose is to facilitate the free flow of suggestions, advice, requests, and information throughout the company.

(1) Facilitate interdepartmental as well as vertical communication and exchange of information.

(2) Collect opinions and ideas from all employees, and use them as a reference for small improvements and innovation.

(3) Use suggestions as points of reference for changing the way work is done in each department.

2 OBJECT

(1) All employees have the freedom to make suggestions to the company and relevant departments.

(2) The company and relevant departments use suggestions as references or hints.

3 SUBMITTING SUGGESTIONS

(1) Clarify the relevant department and submit it into the suggestion box, or give it to a suggestion committee member.

(2) The suggestion committee circulates the suggestions to the relevant department.

4 RESPONSE

(1) No answer is given to the suggester (feedback is provided periodically through company newsletter or memoranda).

(2) No reward is paid in principle for individual suggestions (a reward may be paid on the recommendation from the relevant department).

(3) At its discretion, the suggestion committee may promote special suggestion campaigns to solicit ideas that relate to a particular theme. The committee reserves the right to define time periods, awards, and evaluation methods related to such campaigns.

5 OWNERSHIP

(1) All rights relating to suggestions are reserved by the company.

(2) No one submitting a suggestion may claim responsibility for implemented improvements or for the development or marketing of a new product.

This is because it is difficult to judge the uniqueness of a suggestion. Often, ideas are not as unique as submitters suppose. It is not uncommon for departments to receive several similar ideas from different people. Also, the level of suggestion can vary from a wish to concrete idea for implementation. Nevertheless, in the end credit must go to the person or persons who have actually implemented an improvement. It is up to the department that implemented the improvement to submit a Kaizen report and obtain a reward. It is left to their discretion to decide whether to reward the idea or ideas that may have inspired them to act.

departments and up through levels of management. When you compare the above benefits to those that result from kaizen implementation, however, the gap in importance and thus priority is obvious. You don't have to abandon your suggestion system if you make a clear distinction between it and the kaizen reporting system. To do so is to create a situation in which implemented improvements and suggestions flow freely.

"Have to Do" versus "May Do"

When you compare the objectives of the sample kaizen reporting system to those of the suggestion system, the difference in importance assigned to them by management becomes very clear. In an economic era in which advanced technology, customer service, and quality are increasingly important, in which personnel costs comprise the greatest overhead, and in which human resources determine the fate of the company, the development of the awareness, willingness, and ability of all employees is the most important issue facing managers today.

For this reason, all employees should participate in the kaizen reporting system. Furthermore, management has to take responsibility for the promotion and guidance of the system. It is something that *has* to be tackled with great seriousness, because the company's survival and future is at stake. The suggestion system, on the other hand, can be offered as an option. A company may do it if it wants to, but only if it can do so without expending a great deal of time and energy. For instance, you should not bother to create a separate system for evaluating and marking suggestions.

Evaluating a suggestion is rather like discussing the taste of cake portrayed in a picture or photograph. However realistic the cake appears, it still has no flavor. The effect of an idea can only be discussed once it is implemented. Kaizen reporting makes it possible, figuratively speaking, to try a small piece of the cake before discussing its taste.

28

Give Credit for a Positive Effect to the Person and Department Responsible for Creating It

With suggestions a reward need not be paid, but if one is, ¥100 ($.75) is acceptable. But once the idea is adopted and some benefit is realized, credit must go to the person and the department involved in the implementation. This is acceptable as long as rewards are paid for kaizen reporting, because the majority of ideas and suggestions submitted by outsiders to other departments have almost certainly been considered and tackled before by the parties involved.

Even if a suggested idea is appreciated, the credit for the benefit must go to the person or persons who acknowledged the idea's worth—those who assumed the risk and responsibilities of implementation. Otherwise, the idea never would have seen the light of day. Therefore, it's important to give credit where it's due—to the person who makes a tangible benefit possible. When the implementers' efforts are acknowledged and rewarded, that department will surely look upon suggestions from another department as seeds for kaizen.

On the other hand, if only the idea is evaluated and the person who implements it is *not* compensated—as is the case with traditional suggestion systems—the system is bound to be seen as an interfering hindrance. Furthermore, if an evaluation committee forces a department to implement a suggestion or idea, it will create an impression of itself as an overbearing group of dictators.

Ideas and information tend to flow freely around people and departments with the ability and willingness to evaluate and use these inputs effectively. A clear-sighted person can get a lot of mileage out of even a mediocre idea. Conversely, brilliant ideas go to waste due to incompetence.

Similarly, it is a waste of time to provide or to impose suggestions upon a department that lacks the willingness and skills to implement them. A suggestion system can't do anything to improve such a situation, because the situation reflects more deep-seated organizational problems. It would be covering up managerial negligence with employees' efforts. Although a kaizen teian system is not a cure-all for organizational problems, it does develop the skills that make lasting improvements possible— from the bottom up.

THE KAIZEN SHEET AS A TOOL FOR CONTINUOUS IMPROVEMENT AND SKILL DEVELOPMENT, AND THE TEIAN SHEET AS A TOOL FOR DATA COLLECTION

Now that we've clarified the difference between kaizen and suggestions, we believe it is also important to point out the differences in the forms— i.e., the tools—used for each type of activity. First, the kaizen reporting sheet. This is a report of an implemented improvement of one's own work. With the approval or guidance of a supervisor, people report what they did and the benefit that resulted.

As the form on page 32 shows, the kaizen sheet and the consultation sheet are virtually the same. The difference is that the kaizen sheet is for reporting implemented improvements, and the consultation sheet is for requesting the help of one's supervisor.

The teian—or suggestion—sheet, however, is used to give employees the chance to submit suggestions, recommendations, inquiries, etc. to managers and other departments. To encourage such communication, some companies pay small rewards for suggestions.

- of your own work
- of your worksite

KAIZEN

Reporting Sheet (implementation)
Consultation Sheet (to be implemented)

Date		
Dept. Sect.	Name	Make it simple with diagram and drawing

Title

Benefit

- -

Problem (before kaizen)	Improvement (after kaizen)

	Human resources development (modest reward)		Benefit determines reward	
	Some Benefit	Considerable Benefit	Large Benefit	Upper-grade Evaluation
Effect	¥ 500	¥ 1,000	⟹	¥ 5,000 ¥50,000
Focus	Support and Collaboration	Support and Collaboration	Support and Collaboration	
Awareness	Advice or Guidance	Advice or Guidance	Advice or Guidance	

Comments
Primary evaluation _____ Signature

◎ For first-stage rewards, make a prompt decision, taking into account the skill level of the submitter

◎ For upper-grade rewards of more than ¥5,000, apply for a final evaluation by writing a recommendation for the submitter

- Suggestions
- Information
- Questions
- Advice

TEIAN

Japan HR Association

For Other Departments
For Managers and Executives

Destination (to which Dept. / Section ?)	Date	
	Dept. Section	Name

Title

Benefit

Problem (inconvienience, dissatisfaction)	Suggested Ideas / Advice

Although your "request, information, and advice" will be circulated to the relevant department for reference,

◎ There will be no individual answer nor followup to your suggestion (answers will be periodically summarized)

◎ There will be no individual evaluation or reward (with the recommendation of the receiving department, a reward may be given)

Different Objectives Require Different Tools

Use kaizen sheets to record small break-throughs in the way work is done

Use teian or suggestion sheets to communicate ideas to other departments and upper management

THE KAIZEN REPORTING SYSTEM AND HUMAN RESOURCES DEVELOPMENT

With regard to evaluation and rewards in the kaizen reporting system, we recommend that evaluators make prompt decisions. When the reward is up to ¥1,000 ($7), it serves as an educational investment. The idea is to nurture the company's human resources as much as it is to praise and encourage participation in kaizen activities. We therefore strongly suggest that evaluators make prompt decisions, taking into account a submitter's intentions and skill level.

Remember that the kaizen reporting system is a tool for improving work as well as building enthusiasm and developing skills. It is exactly for this reason that employees must submit their kaizen sheets to their direct supervisors. This fosters the direct communication, consultation, and guidance that results in skill development. As skills increase, so does one's confidence and enthusiasm.

The Value of a Suggestion Depends upon the Ability of the Recipients

The purpose of suggestion systems is to establish smooth internal communication—free exchange of information and ideas. Therefore, if the aim is to maintain interdepartmental freedom of expression, it is best to put teian sheets into a suggestion box, or hand them to someone on the suggestion committee. This ensures that information gets directly to the relevant department, without creating unnecessary friction or interference.

The relevant department then must use its discretion in dealing with the suggestion it has received. Whether the suggestion can be implemented depends on the willingness and ability of the people in that department, rather than on the quality of the idea or information itself. This is why we say the value of a suggestion depends upon the attitude and ability of the recipients.

HOW TO USE SUGGESTIONS WISELY

It is also necessary to clarify that it is best not to respond to individual suggestions. Since there are similar requests and suggestions being made continuously, it is better to give one answer to all of them after collecting them over a period of time.

It is time-consuming to answer each one individually, and there are also many cases where suggestions and advice are too elaborate for a prompt response. In these situations, if evaluators try to respond quickly, they will have to give irrelevant responses such as, "We will consider it," thus trivializing what may in fact be a suggestion of great insight and value. In addition, this may create great distrust between departments and employees. Thus a well-intentioned system may end up causing an adverse effect. Should a company collect and classify suggestions over a period of time, however, it creates an important information resource. Management will be able to track trends in employee suggestions and opinions, thus gaining an understanding of the relative importance that employees assign to a variety of issues and ideas for corporate improvement. When employees' suggestions and ideas are used this way, they provide valuable insights for managers.

Collecting and classifying suggestions also allows for more substantial feedback. Instead of giving separate and brief feedback to everyone who has submitted a similar suggestion, the company may create a detailed response for general distribution. Such a report acknowledges employees' concerns while also demonstrating that what many may have claimed as a unique idea was in fact a common concern.

Bear in mind that a suggestion system often has a purging effect, inducing an explosion of internal dissatisfaction and frustration. This is perfectly acceptable as long as this phase is a short one. Everyone needs to blow off a little steam now and then. Allow this phase to continue indefinitely, however, and most certainly it will create a great deal of negativity in the work environment.

That is why it is often best to focus suggestion activities around particular themes over finite periods of time. This for the most part makes it more difficult to stew over a particular complaint for a long time. It is also a good idea to provide special rewards and evaluation standards for this type of suggestion campaign. To do so encourages clear, straightforward suggestion activity.

KEEP RULES AND
REGULATIONS SIMPLE
AND FLEXIBLE

5

We recommend that when compiling or revising the rules and regulations for a kaizen teian system the following sentence be inserted: "The rules are as shown on the attached page and it is expected that managers and supervisors will demonstrate flexibility in interpreting them." We have seen regulations created by many companies, and most of them are tedious. They have lengthy explanations of minute details, which practically guarantees that no one will read them. We would be willing to bet that even someone actively involved in the promotion of the system would get a headache trying to plow through this stuff!

Usually such documents end up in the archives, which obviously is not a good place for the guidelines for a vital kaizen teian system.

DETAILS SHOULD FIT EASILY ON ONE PAGE

The rules for kaizen activity, which is meant to motivate people to *act*, must be concise enough to fit on a single sheet of paper. If the rules take up more space, people will toss them straight into the wastebasket or into a desk drawer.

We know that those managing and promoting kaizen activities feel compelled to set up solid rules. But they should keep in mind that doing so will have an adverse effect. The longer the rules, the less likely it is that people will read them; the more detailed they are, the more likely it is that they will cause confusion and misunderstanding.

If a company has compiled bulky and grandiose rules, we recommend that they throw them away immediately. Then they should replace the old set with a simple set that will fit onto one side of a single sheet of paper.

In fact, since one of the important principles of kaizen is the elimination of unnecessary work, the kaizen promotion committee can set a good example by eliminating silly and unnecessary rules. There is nothing more ridiculous than appealing to employees for improvement and efficiency with an enormous set of lengthy and verbose rules.

38

DETAILED RULES BOG DOWN THE IMPROVEMENT PROCESS

How do rules get to be so long? Because often they include details relating to management and administration of the system. It is important, therefore, to distinguish between the rules and the administration of them; and to keep them separate.

Make Flexibility a Priority

The worst effect of inserting management details into the rules is that the rules become inflexible, the system becomes less

Tearing up complex rules and regulations helps activate the system

fluid, and therefore improvement becomes rigid and dull. In some companies, the rules include issues as detailed as the number of times per year that the promotional committee decides on the themes for improvement campaigns, the number of people that comprise the promotion committee, the amount of rewards for participation, etc. Including such information only serves to smother kaizen activities.

Such concerns should be addressed as circumstances dictate and with flexibility. Whether improvement and campaigns are necessary, and what their themes and frequency should be, for example, depend on such things as participation rates and the prevailing economic environment.

Any mention of management details should be confined to a simple statement recognizing the promotion committee's intention to address special concerns as they arise.

The object of kaizen teian activities is to engage people's creativity so that they help change old and inefficient methods of work. Such breakthroughs are not possible when those promoting the system have to abide by or enforce a rigid set of rules.

Real kaizen activities start when companies tear up lengthy rules and allow managers and supervisors some freedom.

What Are Rules for Anyway?

Based on experience, we know that many readers will still have doubts. Here are some of the most common ones we have heard:

- "Although you say this is clear enough, (state your specific doubt here) ..."
- "Does it really work with such slack rules?"
- "Don't you think there's a reason why rules have to go into such great detail?"

Don't worry, though. Rules, or the way things should be, always vary according to the objective. So it is necessary to ask: "What are the rules for?"

Our work consists of two aspects: maintaining the status quo and breaking through the status quo. If the rules are meant to maintain the status quo, that is, to do assigned work in a predetermined way, then the details have to be clearly defined.

Details of breaking through the status quo, however, must not be written down, because when we say "breaking through the status quo," we are really talking about progress and development; and we cannot reasonably define that which has no precedent! Therefore, writing down minute details will not—cannot—serve the system. That's why rules for breakthrough activities must be short and simple enough to fit on one sheet of paper. This encourages employee involvement and allows managers the flexibility to respond quickly to special circumstances and changing conditions.

ESTABLISH A STRONG PURPOSE AND REVISE DETAILS WHEN NECESSARY

Any system is a tool, and the kaizen teian system is a means of starting and maintaining continuous improvement. A company must take care to create a system well suited to its objectives and prevailing conditions. Managers must remember, however, that the objectives and conditions may change at any time, which means that kaizen activities will have to change also.

In practice, this means that rules, evaluation standards, reward structures, kaizen sheets, etc., should all be changed as managers deem it necessary to do so. In fact, we recommend that managers review the elements of the kaizen teian system annually in order to ensure that the system is coping with change adequately.

As a consequence of change, of course, one hears expressions of frustration: "Rules change too often." "It's difficult to get used to the system." "What a bother!" Don't be daunted by such comments. It is human nature to resist change. But as long as a company has established a strong purpose and a corresponding policy to support continuous improvement activities, then it is capable of weathering change well.

Managers always encounter opposition and resistance to change, but when the issue is kaizen activity, they must not back down. Otherwise they surely will not be able to cope with change themselves. As long as revisions are consistent with company policy, however, there should be no problem in the long run.

REVISE FOR THE SAKE OF SIMPLICITY

When a system and its rules change frequently, it's usually because a company has done a poor job of defining direction and policy. Naturally this causes confusion and irritation among employees. Unless managers confirm expectations and the main purpose of the kaizen teian system, people end up feeling abused by

41

it. Ridiculous and ill-considered revisions are made without much thought or as the result of incomplete thinking. When one overhears such comments as, "Other companies are doing this," or "This method seems to work," it is a good bet that the company has not established a strong purpose and a clear policy to accompany it.

Complications also arise when various suggestions are put forward at the workplace, and in their eagerness to please everyone, managers make unwise compromises and revisions. This can't be called flexibility, it's just weakness and indecisiveness, and again, it shows that the company's kaizen efforts lack a clear focus.

If on the other hand, a company gets too specific about its purpose, policy takes the form of lots of petty points cited one after another. If this is the case, things get more and more complex every time there is a new revision.

When managers make so many accommodations, rules grow thicker and thicker with each revision, forms get increasingly complex and incomprehensible and become difficult to fill in.

Remember: the spirit of kaizen is simplicity. Therefore, the system should be easy to understand and participate in. Never implement any revision that makes the rules even slightly more complex. This is regression. Encourage instead revision towards simplicity. Do so as much as possible, because this is real kaizen.

ADOPT GUERRILLA TACTICS TO ADVANCE KAIZEN ACTIVITIES

Every company has a unique identity and as a result, unique complications. Managers quickly discover that knowing the theory behind kaizen teian systems is not enough when they attempt to get one started in their own company. Suddenly they confront all kinds of obstacles and get frustrated because it is so hard to change things.

It is to these people we say, don't worry. Overcoming formidable obstacles is in fact a kaizen activity in its own right. If change through innovation is impossible, the kaizen approach of starting where you can, with whatever resources are available, will serve you well.

Managers attempting to activate a kaizen teian system should study the following words and phrases:

- for the time being
- in the meantime
- temporarily
- let's be flexible

Clever managers learn to use these phrases, because, like guerrilla leaders taking on a formidable foe, they understand that the victories are achieved in small steps using unorthodox methods.

One such method is to introduce a kaizen teian system as an experiment within, say, one department. A small success leads to other small successes, which makes it easier to eventually activate a companywide kaizen teian system.

Whenever changes occur throughout a company, resistance and friction are bound to occur. There are always people who will be

- against it anyhow
- against it to start with
- against *anything* new

It is a waste of time to try to deal with such people seriously. It is far quicker to activate a kaizen teian system on a trial basis. Promptness is the strength of kaizen. When clever managers successfully get people involved in kaizen activities with a minimum of argument and discussion, the value of such activities becomes apparent. This is another compelling reason for keeping the rules and the system simple. Simplicity ensures action; action results in tangible positive effect.

Another thing managers have to cope with is the complaint that the system is bad and that the rules must be changed. When

43

this happens managers need to consider whether changing the system and the rules will clear away all the problems. In our experience, this is never true. We cannot stress enough that the system works best when companies embrace a flexible management style and cut out complex rules and regulations.

A Simple Evaluation Standard for First-Stage Kaizen

An example of the first-stage evaluation standard with a reward of up to about ¥1,000 ($7) is shown on page 46. Rewards are only relevant here for kaizen reporting—instances in which improvements have already been implemented and from which the benefit has already been seen.

Of course, in some companies, employees are encouraged to consult with their supervisors about suggested kaizen prior to implementation, so in such cases it is a good idea to have a small amount available for promotion and consultation.

However, since it is only a step towards kaizen implementation, the amount should be less than the amount given for kaizen reporting. In such cases, concreteness is the minimum requirement for suggested kaizen. If the submitter is only pointing out a problem, the supervisor must give some guidance so that the employee can then come up with an improvement suggestion.

Standards for Quick Evaluation

	Human resources development (modest reward)		Benefit determines reward	
	Some Benefit	Considerable Benefit	Large Benefit	Upper-grade Evaluation
Implementing an improvement	¥ 500	¥ 1,000	⟶	¥ 5,000 ¥50,000
Thinking about how to solve problems	Support and Collaboration	Support and Collaboration	Support and Collaboration	
Noticing problems	Advice or Guidance	Advice or Guidance	Advice or Guidance	

It's simple and easy to understand

◎ For first-stage rewards, make a prompt decision, taking into account the skill level of the submitter

◎ For upper-grade rewards of more than ¥5,000, apply for a final evaluation by writing a recommendation for the submitter

Effort award

Encouragement award

Kaizen report award

THERE IS NO NEED TO ORGANIZE THE REWARD SYSTEM BY LEVEL OR TITLE

The evaluation standard shown above gives no indication of levels or titles. It simply shows reward amounts: ¥500 ($3.50) or ¥1,000 ($7).

Many companies set more complex standards that designate several different levels of improvement ideas, but this is not necessary. In fact, it is better to keep things more simple and comprehensible by simply designating awards by amount.

Similarly, it's a bad idea to give irrelevant names to rewards:

- suggestion award
- effort award
- promotional award

Looking at these titles gives no precise sense of their meaning and the worth attached to them. Therefore, people will demand explanations. This makes the standards complicated and eventually leads to misunderstanding and confusion.

With a straightforward indication of the amount, no explanations or names are necessary. It is all very simple to understand. Nevertheless, there may be a feeling that this is a little tasteless, and if this is the case, you should make some kind of obvious distinction between the awards, such as gold, silver, and bronze.

Under no circumstances should deciphering the standards require a detailed key or legend. More detailed standards may be necessary, however, in order to evaluate upper-grade improvements that have been nominated for annual awards.

FIRST-STAGE EVALUATIONS: AN INVESTMENT IN HUMAN RESOURCES

For first-stage evaluations with rewards of up to ¥1,000 ($7), we do not recommend an evaluation standard based on conventional marking methods (see *Kaizen Teian 1*, chapter 8 for further details). This is a complete waste.

Evaluation at this stage is somewhat subjective, and this is as it should be. The purpose of first-stage evaluation is educational investment—to praise and encourage people for what they have done to improve the way they do their work. So, strict marking has no real meaning. In addition, it is often very difficult to perceive objectively the benefit gained from kaizen at this level.

Because human resource development is an important objective at this stage, when a direct supervisor evaluates an improvement proposal, he or she is likely to be less concerned with the bottom-line benefit than the idea's worth relative to the skill level of the person who submitted it. Do not worry too much about the fairness of individual evaluations. It's natural for the evaluation of similar improvement ideas to vary according to the degree of need or urgency and the level of skill demonstrated by those who have submitted ideas. You can correct for overlenient or overstringent evaluation over time by reviewing overall and statistical distributions.

It is foolish, however, to second-guess a direct supervisor's evaluation. What is gained by assigning a highly paid senior manager to carry out kaizen evaluation, the reward for which is a mere ¥1,000 ($7)? This is playing games. Not only is it a waste of time, but such second-guessing will discourage supervisors' willingness and commitment.

In companies that have adopted a detailed marking method, one often hears the following comments:

- "Evaluation standards are ambiguous."
- "Evaluation standards must be more detailed."

In our experience, however, the people who make such comments are never satisfied. The more detailed you make the standards, the more detail they want.

Conversely, if the system emphasizes simple standards and quick decision making—things that would seem to contribute to ambiguity—strangely enough, nobody will comment that standards are ambiguous. This is because judgment is left to the evaluators, and the prompt method of judgment demands standards of the evaluators themselves. When given a responsibility, people tend to take the initiative in demonstrating their ability to make judgments.

"WE SHALL CONSIDER IT"

The major demerit of the traditional suggestion system is the abuse of such words as, "I shall consider it" or "put on hold." Such things are unavoidable with the traditional suggestion system, though, because people are only supposed to submit ideas and requests, and it is the suggestion committee's role to take them into consideration. Furthermore, upper management also examines and judges the suggestions. So when employees are told, "We shall consider it" or "It's under consideration," it means they are unlikely to get feedback for a *long* time.

NO CONSIDERATION REQUIRED

With the kaizen reporting system, careful thought takes place at the workplace—the place where the improvement ideas originate. Employees ask,

- "Why is this problem occurring?"
- "What is the root cause of the problem?"
- "What if we did this as a countermeasure?"
- "Will the countermeasure cause additional problems?"

Asking such questions and finding answers to them—often with the help of one's supervisor and colleagues—results in implemented improvements. The kaizen report confirms benefits. The results are there for all to see, so there is no need for further consideration.

What is needed is judgment. Evaluation therefore becomes a matter of deciding how much to pay for the kaizen report. And the decision is one that needs to be made in seconds. The kaizen teian system places the responsibility for making such judgments on the shoulders of the submitter's immediate supervisor—the person who knows both the job and the submitter better than anyone else in the company.

By weighing the value of the improvement and the skill level of the submitter, the supervisor should be able to decide in seconds whether to award ¥500 ($3.50) or ¥1,000 ($7). If the supervisor cannot make this decision, it is likely that he or she is confused about the relationship between judgment and consideration.

PRINCIPLES OF
UPPER-GRADE EVALUATIONS

Here are some of the comments we hear most often regarding upper-grade evaluations:

- We hesitate to make decisions on whether to recommend improvements for upper-grade evaluations. Please clarify some standards for making such decisions.
- Although our section has never applied for an upper-grade evaluation, another section, which implemented an idea similar to one of ours, did apply; and the person who implemented the idea received a greater reward. It was very hard to explain to the employee in our section why this happened.

Generally speaking, there is an element of subjectivity to the kaizen teian system that makes such concerns likely. This is because the system is action-oriented and flexible. Therefore, it sacrifices absolute certainties for the sake of speed and simplicity. Nevertheless, we think we can address these concerns by stressing the importance of the supervisor's role in the kaizen teian system and clarifying the difference between first-stage and upper-grade evaluations.

SUPERVISORS MUST ADVOCATE FOR THE PEOPLE WHO IMPLEMENT IMPROVEMENTS

The key player, the person best able to decide whether an idea is worthy of an upper-grade reward, is the submitter's direct supervisor. If the supervisor believes that an improvement is worthy of an upper-grade evaluation, he or she should not hesitate to write a recommendation for the person who implemented the idea. If the supervisor judges that the improvement does not rate an upper-grade evaluation, then he or she offers thanks, words of encouragement, and a reward of either ¥500 ($3.50) or ¥1,000 ($7). In either case, the greatest responsibility for the evaluation of improvements rests with the direct supervisor—the person most familiar with the work of the people in a particular section or department.

WHAT IS THE DIFFERENCE BETWEEN A FIRST-STAGE AND AN UPPER-GRADE IMPROVEMENT?

Upper-grade rewards may be anywhere from ¥5,000 ($35) to several tens of thousands of yen. So the question arises: How is the amount of the reward determined? Basically, even upper-grade evaluations take place in a hop-skip-jump method: rewards jump from ¥5,000 ($35) to, say, ¥7,000 ($50), then ¥10,000 ($70), etc. Aside from the amount of the reward, how, then, is an upper-grade evaluation different from a first-stage evaluation?

The difference lies in the reward's emphasis. Rewards of up to ¥1,000 ($7) are educational investments—investments in human resource development. Rewards of ¥5,000 ($35) and higher reflect the benefit realized as a result of implementing an improvement idea. We suggest the following simple standard for making a distinction between first-stage and upper-grade evaluations:

1. With rewards up to ¥1,000 ($7), an objective measurement of the benefit is not necessary. Just a quick, subjective evaluation is enough. There is no need for an elaborate marking system.
2. Tangible benefits determine the value of upper-grade rewards. Therefore, a marking system based on the actual benefit is necessary.

The Difference between a First-Stage and an Upper-Grade Evaluation

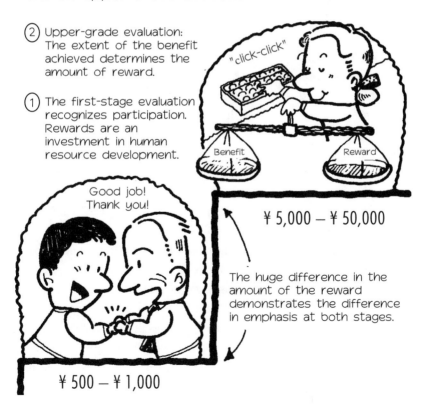

② Upper-grade evaluation: The extent of the benefit achieved determines the amount of reward.

① The first-stage evaluation recognizes participation. Rewards are an investment in human resource development.

"click-click"

Benefit

Reward

Good job! Thank you!

¥ 5,000 – ¥ 50,000

The huge difference in the amount of the reward demonstrates the difference in emphasis at both stages.

¥ 500 – ¥ 1,000

3. Applications for upper-grade rewards must include a benefit description.

We would like to emphasize an important point: In both first-stage and upper-grade evaluation, judgment is the responsibility of the submitter's direct supervisor. The supervisor either decides on the spot to reward up to ¥1,000 ($7), or recommends the idea—providing the proper documentation—for an upper-grade reward. A final evaluation then takes place.

FINAL EVALUATIONS ARE REALLY JUST A MEANS OF CHECKING

It is also necessary to clarify that the final evaluation for upper-grade rewards, usually conducted by an award committee, is really just a checking structure. A company determines the criteria that makes different ideas worth specific amounts of money, say ¥5,000 ($35), ¥10,000 ($70), ¥15,000 ($100), and so on. The direct supervisor judges not only whether an improvement is worthy of a first-stage or upper-grade reward, but, if the idea is worthy of an upper-grade reward, he or she decides its monetary value and justifies the decision in a recommendation to the award committee. The committee's role is not to re-evaluate the improvement idea or second-guess the supervisor; it is simply to check that the reward is appropriate compared to the benefit achieved.

Often rewards between ¥1,000 ($7) and ¥10,000 ($70) are considered middle-grade rewards. Usually, any member of the award committee is authorized to approve rewards of less than ¥10,000 ($70) and people receive their money fairly quickly. Even with upper-grade rewards, the committee usually is able to make a decision no later than one month from the time of the supervisor's recommendation. In both cases, the recommendation is necessary. It is for this reason that the success of a kaizen teian system depends a great deal upon the eagerness and commitment of supervisors.

PART

T

W

O

HOW TO USE THE
KAIZEN SHEET AS A TOOL

Filling in the kaizen sheet is not an end in itself; it is a tool used to improve work, a powerful device with which to objectively grasp and solve problems. Supervisors also find that the kaizen sheet is an invaluable resource for developing people and guiding implementation of improvements.

FROM UNCONSCIOUS IMPROVEMENT TO CONSCIOUS IMPROVEMENT

There are people who worry that activating kaizen reporting is difficult. We commonly hear: "We could barely cope with the conventional improvement proposal system in which all kaizen was welcome. I don't think a company of our level can manage it."

Nothing could be further from the truth. In reality, the kaizen reporting system is far easier. Twelve kaizen items per person per year—i.e., one a month—can be achieved with ease. Companies that deal mainly with implemented kaizen have already shown this to be true. In fact, they are often surprised to find that after just one month they have received as many as five or six implemented improvements per person.

Uncover Improvements that Have Already Been Implemented

Here are some of the fears common to companies contemplating activation of a kaizen reporting system:

- "It's difficult."
- "It will reduce the number of improvements submitted."
- "It will reduce levels of participation."

A common preconception is that kaizen reporting involves Herculean efforts followed by written reports. This is not so. In reality, in any workplace a fair amount of improvements have already been implemented. The kaizen reporting system capitalizes on this basic fact. There is absolutely no need to "create" new improvements. All that's necessary is to write down the improvements that have already been implemented, and in no time it's possible to identify five or six.

This is the first step of the kaizen reporting system—digging out the improvements that have been made randomly and unconsciously and revealing them for what they are. Doing so helps make the process of implementing improvements a conscious rather than unconscious one—one that people tackle continuously with commitment.

Joint Ownership of Kaizen

Once you have uncovered improvements implemented unconsciously, it is a good idea to collate the kaizen reports and compile them in an example booklet. The objective is both to inform and inspire people. When they see practical examples of improvements, people begin to appreciate that there are simple things one can do to transcend perceived limitations within a particular work environment.

Success breeds success. Documenting simple solutions to common problems therefore leads to joint ownership of future improvements. People see not only that it is possible to solve problems, but they also get fairly detailed descriptions of how they were solved. As they model their own improvements after the ones seen in the example booklet, they begin thinking in terms of "we" rather than "I." In other words, they begin to think: "This is what *we* did to improve *our* work."

USE UNCONSCIOUSLY IMPLEMENTED IMPROVEMENTS AS A RUNWAY FOR FUTURE IMPROVEMENTS

To summarize, improvement activities progress smoothly provided that

1. people write up unconsciously implemented improvements in kaizen reports
2. the company compiles a simple booklet of examples

The experience of documenting unconsciously implemented improvements is highly instructive. It provides an opportunity to carefully analyze the steps involved both in defining problems and in solving them.

As people familiarize themselves with the process of defining and solving problems—and as they see examples of improvements that others have implemented—their awareness expands. They begin to see opportunities for improvement that they had not previously considered; they begin to apply good ideas from the examples they have seen to their own work; and they begin to see that problems have more than one solution.

We learn from our own successes and create the next opportunity to implement improvements. This is the greatest power of the kaizen reporting system, and this is the effect that only kaizen reporting can bring. Learning from unconsciously implemented improvements allows people to extract the subsequent conscious kaizen with ease. It is rather like a plane on a runway: Through the process of writing down the improvements you have already implemented, you can "take off" with the next improvement easily and naturally.

Use Existing Improvements as a Runway

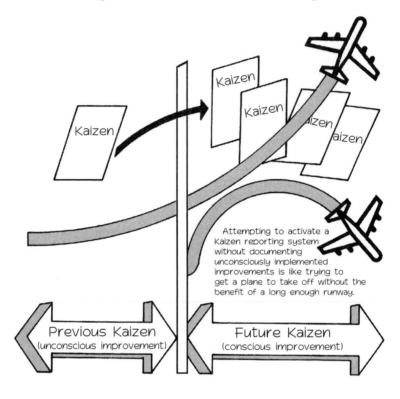

Attempting to activate a Kaizen reporting system without documenting unconsciously implemented improvements is like trying to get a plane to take off without the benefit of a long enough runway.

Previous Kaizen
(unconscious improvement)

Future Kaizen
(conscious improvement)

Don't Search for Treasure That's Buried under Your Feet

Some companies attempt to activate the kaizen reporting system by purchasing and studying a number of textbooks on improvement techniques or attending seminars with difficult themes. Of course, these texts and the training are not a complete waste; it's better to possess some knowledge than none. However, the benefit gained will not be proportional to the cost and time invested.

To study improvement techniques and examples through textbooks and seminars is to gain knowledge but not wisdom. Wisdom can only be gained as a result of one's own experience.

Isn't it foolish for companies to look elsewhere for treasure that's buried right under their feet? Kaizen activities require no special talent or skill, just common sense and normal ability. You don't have to look outside to learn how to make improvements. The process of documenting unconsciously implemented improvements in kaizen reports teaches the know-how necessary to make the kaizen reporting system fly.

PUT SMALL IMPROVEMENTS IN THE SPOTLIGHT

Those who resist activating a kaizen reporting system say:

- "That might work in other companies, but not in a place like ours."
- "Our employees are so stubborn. They won't think about kaizen because they don't think about anything. And you want me to have them write reports? No way!"

In our experience, when managers assume that their employees are somehow inadequate or stubborn, it says more about the managers than it does about the employees.

Even in badly managed companies, though, remarkable things may happen when people start the first phase of kaizen reporting. They realize that they have implemented improvements unconsciously by thinking about how they do their work. It is only because the employees have never been made conscious of improvement—it has never been recognized or acknowledged—that kaizen activities have previously failed to be a driving force.

When unconsciously implemented improvements are revealed, praised, acknowledged, evaluated, and rewarded, improvement activities can become a driving force.

Contrary to innovation, which requires special ability and professional skills, kaizen reporting requires no special skills. With management support, any company can begin to cultivate an improvement-oriented environment.

In the first stage of kaizen reporting, a great number of the reports will be more or less incomplete. Don't be discouraged. Remember that the improvements have been implemented unconsciously. People are still learning what's required—and finding clues to conscious kaizen in the process.

Even improvements that provoke a reaction of "Is this it?" or "That's nothing out of the ordinary" must be considered and evaluated at the first stage. The purpose of this stage is to build a foundation for continuous improvement, and managers and supervisors can do this by putting the spotlight on improvement that might be thought of as trivial or petty. In reality, however, there is no such thing as a trivial or petty improvement.

EASING ANXIETIES ABOUT
DOCUMENTING IMPROVEMENTS

There is a crucial mistake managers and supervisors need to avoid when activating the kaizen reporting system or changing to it from a traditional suggestion system. The worst thing a manager or supervisor can do in either case is to pressure employees to submit improvements.

DEMANDING PEOPLE TO WRITE AND SUBMIT IMPROVEMENTS BACKFIRES

Demanding that people write and submit improvements gives the impression that they have to produce something new. They will feel obliged to submit something out of the ordinary, so they will simply stare at the sheet, and say:

- "It's difficult."
- "I can't write anything."
- "I am not capable."

The more they feel pressured to submit clever ideas, the more they will resist putting anything in writing. There's no faster way to sabotage the kaizen reporting system.

"Try to Write It Down" Is a More Natural Approach

Instead of pressuring employees to write and submit kaizen, supervisors should try using the following phrases:

- "Please write your improvement on a kaizen sheet."
- "Try to write down what you have already done."

Simple as they seem, such approaches are much more effective. Some people might say there's no difference. We disagree. Why? Asking someone politely to write something down suggests that he or she only needs to put into words improvements that already exist. Therefore, there is no implication that it is necessary to produce something new or ingenious. The more polite phrases above remind employees that they only need to write about the improvements that they have already implemented.

Remind People That the Thinking Part Happens While They Are Working

As we suggested above, employees' greatest anxiety comes from the belief that they are required to come up with brilliant ideas out of nowhere. They sit in front of the kaizen sheet, agonizing like great authors trying to squeeze out a fantastic story onto a blank sheet of paper.

This is why it is important for supervisors to remind people that there is no need to think deeply or think of anything new when the kaizen sheet is before them. The thinking part happens when people are working. Who, when they are working, isn't aware of problems or things they would like to change? Furthermore, who hasn't, at one time or another, implemented some small improvement to make work easier? The objective is to make people more aware of the small things they do—or wish to do—in order to make their work easier. In this way, people will make a transition from unconscious kaizen to conscious kaizen.

Supervisors should remind people that when writing kaizen reports they have only to stick to the simple facts that show what they have already thought about and accomplished.

KAIZEN STARTS WHEN PEOPLE DOCUMENT THEIR IMPROVEMENTS

Keeping a diary is something anyone can do, so it may be helpful to think of kaizen reporting as keeping a continuous improvement diary. People make a note of the improvements they have implemented that day, that week, or that month. Indeed, they report any changes they have made in their work and even problems that may require the attention of a small group to solve.

But the emphasis is on reporting what has already been done, because doing so makes implemented improvement conspicuous. The context of the improvement becomes visible and easy for everyone to see. Then the supervisor can acknowledge and praise the improvement items and also give advice and guidance.

When a supervisor evaluates an improvement and rewards an employee with even a small amount of money, it shows that the company officially recognizes the employee's efforts. In addition, having a written record of the implemented improvement serves a highly practical purpose. The original submitter as well as his or her colleagues may refer to it as an example of how to fill out a kaizen report; or they may refer to it for inspiration—and think of related improvements or refinements. In any case, we've seen time and again that when people submit their first kaizen reports, it as if they have cleared a hurdle. Subsequent reports of improvements are bound to follow.

65

We'd like to end this chapter by showing you a page that one company attaches to their kaizen teian system manual.

Please Report Your Implemented Improvements on the **KAIZEN** Sheet

If you are the kind of person who grumbles about having to write and submit Kaizen reports, or if you are the kind of person who sits staring at the Kaizen sheet, we'd like to make the following recommendation: Please don't take the process so seriously!

We know you work hard. We know you think about your work and make improvements as you go along. So you don't need to think about any new and brilliant ideas when you sit down in front of a blank Kaizen sheet. Just try to write about the way you changed your work.

Furthermore, you don't need to fill in all the sections at once. If you insist on doing it this way it will surely become a burden. If you fill in the problem section or the benefit section as you become aware of problems and benefits, however, you will fill up Kaizen sheets before you know it.

Think of it this way: Every day while you work you unconsciously fill in the blanks on the Kaizen sheet. In your daily work various difficult and unpleasant problems crop up, and one by one you solve them, don't you? The purpose of the Kaizen sheet is to clarify for yourself, your supervisor, your fellow employees, and even managers the ways that you have already improved your job.

A single Kaizen sheet provides you with a work record; a collection of Kaizen sheets represents the accumulation of your improvement know-how. Writing things down on the Kaizen sheet gives you insight into the way you do your work, and subsequently, you're bound to find clues for additional improvements.

Remember: Kaizen is not about creating things. Changing the way you do your work is what it is about. Kaizen means changing things to achieve a more pleasant, efficient, and safe work environment. Improvements can be made in any job. Wherever there is work there is Kaizen.

Priming the
Improvement Pump

ompanies often ask us:

- "Why should we insist that people report improvements they have already implemented?"
- "Why should we reward improvements that have already been implemented?"

Some managers reason that the time it takes to report previously implemented improvements would be better spent implementing new improvements. Another concern is the expense. Some people feel it's simply wasteful to reward improvements that have already been implemented. As we have suggested in the last two chapters, insisting that people report improvements they have already implemented strengthens improvement consciousness. Reinforcing the process by offering rewards is not just a good idea, it's an investment that is likely to pay increasing returns as the people within a company commit themselves to the process of continuous improvement.

Don't Economize on the "Priming Water"

When companies reward people for submitting reports of improvement they have already implemented, the company is not doing so out of kindness. Rewards are an investment in the company's long-term success. If a company is short-sighted, it might consider it wasteful to pay a reward for improvements that have already been implemented. Such companies are satisfied more or less with present conditions and see no cause to bother with rewards.

But most companies want to create instead an improvement-oriented culture. Such companies do not settle for sporadically and unconsciously implemented improvements. They seek to draw upon people's creativity and natural inclination for improvement; they seek to make improvement a deliberate and continuous process.

Giving rewards for improvements already implemented is like priming a pump to induce the flow of subsequent improvements. If a company does not prime the pump adequately it simply won't be able to tap the wellspring of creativity that makes ongoing improvement possible.

Therefore, in the early stages of kaizen reporting, a company should pay rewards generously, even for improvements that appear to be incomplete or insignificant. Supervisors shouldn't be too picky at this stage. They should have faith instead in people's ability to improve even their improvements! People want to improve. With the right encouragement and advice it is almost certain that even if a person's first attempt at kaizen is somehow lacking, he or she will come up with more substantial improvements on subsequent occasions.

And this is what the kaizen system aims for. The object is to tap people's willingness to make improvements and to cultivate this tendency as a habit. The best way to reinforce this willingness is to reward people for submitting reports of the improvements they have implemented. As they document their improvements they think more carefully about their work, which suggests additional improvements. Soon kaizen becomes a habit.

USING THE KAIZEN
SHEET TO UNDERSTAND
PROBLEMS CLEARLY

The kaizen reporting system requires people to act in ways that make improvements possible. Managers, supervisors, and workers may understand the theory behind the system; they may understand why it is necessary to document improvements that have already been implemented; and they may understand why it is necessary to reward such efforts. But when most companies attempt to activate a kaizen reporting system, they quickly discover that understanding the theory behind the system does not guarantee adherence to it. "I'm no good at writing," some people protest. Or: "It's such a hassle to fill out the kaizen sheet; I don't have the time."

As we've said before, true kaizen involves implementation. In order to implement improvements, people must understand how to solve problems. And in order to solve problems, people must understand them clearly. It is impossible, then, to overemphasize the importance of completing kaizen sheets, because they provide a means of doing just that. In this chapter we explore ways to overcome people's resistance to filling out the forms.

What Does It Take to Implement an Improvement?

To say "I understand the problem" may mean little within the context of a kaizen reporting system. "I understand the problem" may really only mean "I am aware of the problem." Real understanding occurs when people begin showing what is needed to implement an improvement and a practical method for doing it.

This is where kaizen reporting differs significantly from improvement campaigns that take place within suggestion systems. With the kaizen reporting system, the actual status of what was improved, how it was improved, and to what extent it was improved is very clear. And it is exactly for this reason that people must fill out their kaizen sheets.

There are always people who can't or won't understand why it is necessary to complete the kaizen sheets. It's a waste of time to explain. Better that supervisors should urge them to have faith that filling out the sheets is a crucial part of the improvement process—that they will learn valuable things as they go along. Even if people think they understand a problem, if they can't put their understanding into practice, it is the same as if they understood nothing. In short, the improvement process is only truly understood when people participate in implementation. The kaizen sheet is the means.

It's Difficult to Fill in a Blank Sheet

What kind of approach should supervisors take with people who complain that it is a hassle to fill in the kaizen sheet?

Such people reject everything at this first stage, because the most difficult thing in the world is to overcome one's initial resistance. It is said that even authors who have written a number of best sellers sometimes struggle to find the first line of a new book.

A Blank Kaisen Sheet Can be Very Intimidating

So it is natural for people to stumble at the start, even with a simple thing like a kaizen report.

Any kaizen sheet has a simple three-part structure: problem, improvement, and benefit. Although people must fill in all three parts or sections in order to submit a kaizen report, there is no rule that says all of the sections have to be completed at the same time. Supervisors should explain this to people, because it will help to alleviate some of the anxiety they feel.

START WITH THE EASIEST SECTION

We recommend to those who shy away from writing kaizen and those who are not accustomed to it that they fill in one section of the kaizen sheet at a time. It's best to start with the easiest section.

Focus on the Problem

Everyone is aware of problems in the workplace. People should think of the negative things that bother, irritate, or even disgust them, and they should write these down as problems. In fact, once people know that it's okay to start this way, they often fill in the problem section of five or six sheets without stopping! Once they complete this first section, the rest comes easily, and strangely enough, kaizen reporting ceases to be a hassle.

This is because the psychological resistance has been eliminated. People get tense in front of an empty sheet of paper, but they seem to relax once one section is filled in. They actually feel like filling in the other empty spaces.

Writing down the problem gets the brain working. Kaizen does not requires innovative ideas—common sense is all that is required. When people make the effort to summarize problems, sometimes possible solutions present themselves as if by magic: "That's it—it might work!"

Even if this doesn't happen, it never hurts to generate a lot of ideas. As soon as a concrete problem is input into the consciousness, the brain starts working. The more problems people write about, the more precisely they tend to identify them. Sometimes the expression of a single problem is too abstract for the mind to grasp, and it is difficult to generate a solution.

For example, what solution exists to the following problem: "I don't like the way the company is set up." The problem is so enormous that it is difficult to find even a clue to a suitable improvement. On the other hand, if we ask, "What aspects of the company don't you like? Write down clear answers on five or six kaizen sheets," we would expect to get the following answers:

74

- "There is too much overtime."
- "It is difficult to take holidays."
- "Meetings go on for too long."
- "Internal communication isn't good."

- "There are too many conferences."

Breaking down the problem into more concrete elements gives the mind food for thought. Using multiple kaizen sheets helps in this process.

The Kaizen Sheet Encourages Precise Thinking

As the example of the kaizen sheet on page 32 shows, limited space is available for filling in the problem. This is a perfect example of the well-known saying that form follows function. Long, elegant reports are of no practical use in determining tangible solutions to problems. What's needed is precision; what's

The Kaizen Reporting System
Encourages Specificity

KAIZEN Reporting (already implemented)
Consultation (to be implemented)

- of your own work
- of your worksite

Title

Benefit

Problem (before Kaizen)

Improvement (after Kaizen)

Make the problem tangible

Think of a concrete improvement idea

needed is a tool that helps people perceive problems clearly and express them concretely. Only when people have defined problems precisely can they truly understand them and begin to generate possible solutions.

The kaizen sheet is a useful tool not only for submitters, but also for supervisors who give guidance and support. Once the problem is written up, the rest is easy. Naturally, clues for advice present themselves clearly; and since the problem is presented and summarized in a concrete way, discussions go smoothly and quickly.

SUPERVISORS MAY FILL IN THE PROBLEM SECTION

Another way of completing the sheet is to have the supervisor fill in the problem section. He or she writes down a problem on a kaizen sheet, photocopies it, and distributes a copy to everyone. It's also very effective to write each person's name on his or her copy.

The purpose of this is to ask everybody to be aware of the problem and to obtain their assistance in solving it. People may have heard about the problem hundreds of times. In fact, they may be sick of hearing about it! "Not that endless preaching again!" they think to themselves.

People react differently when instead of hearing about the problem, they receive their own kaizen sheet on which the problem is clearly defined. They look at the problem; they look at their name on the top of the sheet; and then they begin to consider the problem theirs. If the problem is elementary enough, it may even result in an instant solution.

Even if the problem is the very same one that was spoken about many times before, there is a completely different kind of response. This is because writing the problem on the kaizen sheet makes it explicit. Moreover, only the problem is filled in, leaving the improvement and benefit sections blank. This engages the mind in a way that examining a report that only enumerates problems does not.

"How Many Unfinished Kaizen Sheets Do You Have?

Managers and supervisors tend to use abstract words and phrases, such as "be aware of the problem." In fact, people have heard such expressions so frequently that they cease to mean anything. "Right," people think, "problem awareness," and they carry on with whatever they happen to be doing and don't give it another thought. In companies that have become adept at kaizen reporting, you never hear such meaningless phrases. Instead they will ask the employees, "How many unfinished sheets do you have?" "How many forms do you have with just the problem section completed?"

The purpose of asking such questions is to see how many problems have become tangible. To write a problem on a kaizen sheet is more than problem awareness. It means that someone has a good enough understanding of a particular problem to be able to express it clearly and concisely. As long as the problem is defined clearly, the chances of implementing some kind of improvement are great.

THE VALUE OF STARTING WITH THE BENEFIT SECTION

Although many companies use the method of writing down the problem first, there is in fact a quicker and faster technique, which is to fill in the benefit section first. Just as with the method where people fill in the problem section first, the precondition is that the improvement must already have been implemented.

Similarly, the technique of filling in the benefit section first will not work if supervisors insist that people fill in the remaining sections right away. Some supervisors reason that people should be able to fill in all the sections at once. "Relax," they say to their subordinates, "it's just like keeping a diary." This is no comfort, however, to people who have never kept a diary.

Essentially, what works best is to have employees fill in the section they find easiest. Since the person who implemented the improvement has undoubtedly already experienced its benefit or effect, documenting this fact is an excellent way to begin filling out the kaizen sheet.

Just doing so will take away quite a bit of the psychological resistance people have to beginning the kaizen sheet. Then as they look at the blank sections for problems and improvements, they automatically begin to compare the new, improved situation to the previous, problematic situation. This facilitates the completion of the kaizen report.

A Positive Tool
for Employee
Development
and Evaluation

[12]

The desire to create an improvement-oriented environment motivates companies to activate kaizen reporting systems. Managers and supervisors should be aware, however, that activating a kaizen reporting system requires a change in both routine and attitude. Prior to activation of the kaizen system, for example, a supervisor is essentially an authority figure—someone who issues directives. Under the kaizen reporting system, however, the supervisor's role changes. He or she is expected to act as a coach or adviser.

In this chapter we discuss the ways that the kaizen reporting system enables managers and supervisors to act effectively in accordance with their new roles. The illustration on page 80 summarizes the different methods for using the kaizen sheet as a tool and the benefits gained as a result.

Use of the Kaizen Sheet as a Tool

- of your own work
- of your worksite

KAIZEN

Reporting (already implemented)
Consulting (to be implemented)

Title

Benefit

(1) A tool for documenting unconscious kaizen

(2) A tool for highlighting improvements already implemented

(3) A tool for focusing on strengths rather than faults

(4) A tool for fact-based evaluations

Problem (before Kaizen)

(1) A tool to sort out problems

(2) A tool for understanding problems clearly

(3) A tool for sharing problems

(4) A tool for "digging out" problems

Improvement (after Kaizen)

(1) A tool for coming up with concrete ideas

(2) A tool for expressing ideas that can be implemented

(3) A tool for guidance and advice

(4) A tool to implement improvement ideas

A superlative tool, indeed!

Make good use of it!

80

A BETTER APPROACH TO MOTIVATION AND TRAINING

Under the kaizen reporting system, managers and supervisors coach and advise people, point out problems and opportunities for improvement, evaluate kaizen reports, pay rewards, and make recommendations for upper-grade rewards.

In effect, managers and supervisors are continuously reviewing both the unconscious and the conscious ways that people improve their work. In either case, they reward people for their initiative rather than for simply following orders; and when people are rewarded for assuming more responsibility for their own work, it's almost certain they will be motivated to implement additional improvements.

In the process, as people continue to implement improvements, they develop personally and professionally. Good managers and supervisors make it possible for people to motivate themselves to learn and grow.

SUPERVISORS MUST LOOK FOR IMPROVEMENTS IMPLEMENTED UNCONSCIOUSLY

It's human nature to look for better ways of doing things, so to a certain extent, everybody makes improvements to their work without being aware that they have done so. This is what we call unconscious kaizen. Another common occurrence is when people are aware of making improvements but do not feel they merit mention. "This can't be kaizen," they say. Or: "This isn't worth submitting," and "I'd be embarrassed to submit this."

For the above reasons, supervisors must take it upon themselves to

- discover improvements that people have implemented unconsciously

- point out that there is no such thing as an unworthy implemented improvement

After discovering the improvements that their subordinates have failed to recognize and those that they don't think are worthy of being mentioned, supervisors should encourage people to complete kaizen reports.

It does not really matter how small the improvements are. Supervisors should simply point out the ways in which the improvements have had beneficial effects. By keeping a close eye on their subordinates' work and praising their improvement efforts rather than pointing out faults all the time, supervisors create a foundation for further and more advanced improvement activities.

Supervisors provide two basic types of positive reinforcement. First, they give or recommend financial rewards for improvements that have been implemented and documented. We have never known anyone to complain about receiving an award! Second, supervisors provide praise and encouragement. In our experience, this is perhaps the best motivator there is to ensure high levels of participation in improvement activities. It simply makes people feel good when supervisors show an active interest in the work of individuals.

A TOOL FOR FACT-BASED EVALUATION

There used to be a popular management method known as "smile and tap." The idea was to communicate human warmth. A manager might smile at someone and give him or her a pat on the back for "a job well done"; or perhaps the manager would drape an arm around someone's shoulders. Although the idea of showing human warmth is not a bad one in theory, in practice it often comes across as insincere. Aside from this fact, heightened concern about sexual harassment in the workplace creates ambiguity about what kinds of physical contact might be appropriate.

In the kaizen reporting system, it's possible to show concern and give praise without any type of physical contact. Supervisors and managers look for improvements that their subordinates have implemented and evaluate them based simply on the results. There may be no greater pleasure for employees than knowing that they are receiving real, fact-based evaluations from their supervisors rather than insincere flattery.

In management seminars these days it's often said that managers need to be able to focus on their subordinates' good points instead of their bad points. But this is easier said than done. After all, managers are human, and it's simply not reasonable to expect that a manager or supervisor will be able to relate well to all his or her subordinates. Some people you get along with, others you don't.

What's needed is a more objective tool for focusing on an employee's positive points. In the kaizen reporting system, when supervisors evaluate their employees, they focus on facts—implemented improvements. Although supervisors take into account the relative skill level of the submitter, personality or personal feelings do not affect the evaluation process. As a result, it is entirely possible for supervisors to give praise even to employees with whom they don't relate well on a personal level. Indeed, involvement in improvement activities may very well build common ground between people who otherwise have little in common.

A TOOL FOR FOCUSING ON STRENGTHS RATHER THAN WEAKNESSES

Aside from personality issues, it is always a good idea, whether managers and supervisors relate well to employees or not, to focus on employees' strengths rather than their weaknesses. Generally speaking, though, supervisors and managers tend to focus on their subordinates' faults. This is just the way it is; and the more strongly managers and supervisors feel about their responsibilities, the more they tend to spot the faults of their employees. So, lots of companies and lots of managers pay lip service to adopting systems for "positive" evaluation, but few have come up with a way to actually do it.

The kaizen reporting system provides the means. When supervisors evaluate employees under this system, they are focusing initially on a positive fact: an implemented improvement. Even if the employee's effort is incomplete, the willingness for improvement or the potential for improvement, or both, still exist. In any case, it's always true that in the kaizen reporting system, supervisors focus on employees' strengths. This builds a strong foundation for human resource development.

A Tool for Focusing on Employees' Strengths

EXPERIENCE IS THE BEST TEACHER

People really only come to understand things with certainty as a result of their own experience.

At kaizen seminars held by the Japan Human Relations Association, we lead representatives from different companies through an exercise in which they write down all the improvements that they have implemented in their places of work. After about ten minutes, we then ask them to submit kaizen reports of some of these improvements. Before taking part in this exercise, many people are doubtful about the value of formalizing improvement activities.

Not surprisingly, after they complete the exercise, we commonly hear the following comments:

- "Kaizen means changing the way we do our work. There's opportunity for improvement with any job."
- "Hey, we've been making improvements, and we didn't even realize it!"
- "There's still a lot more we could do with this."
- "This is a good way to enhance communication within our company."
- "We can use this system to create a climate for improvement."

If these are the kinds of reactions we get at a seminar, imagine what happens as companies begin activating kaizen reporting systems.

Just as representatives from various companies developed enthusiasm for the kaizen reporting system after participating in a simple exercise, so will most employees embrace improvement activities once they have firsthand experience implementing their own improvements. In addition, because employees develop new skills in the process of implementing improvements, participation in improvement activities proves to be a particularly effective kind of on-the-job training. This is just another example showing that experience really is the best teacher.

THE SYSTEM IS A TOOL, NOT AN END IN ITSELF

Skeptics are sure to point out that successfully completing a simple exercise at a seminar is no guarantee that a company will be able to activate a kaizen reporting system. They are, of course, correct. But companies *will* have great success activating a kaizen reporting system as long as they remember that it is a means to an end, not an end in itself. We know of a simple case study that illustrates this point quite clearly.

At a conference of kaizen teian promoters from many different companies, one representative from a manufacturing plant—*Company A*—gave the following report:

It's been ridiculously busy lately. The design department in particular has been working overtime every day, and there is no time for kaizen. Please excuse us for only submitting 12 implemented improvements.

Then a representative from a similar type of business—*Company B*—stood up and said:

People in our plant are also busy. The design department also works late, but we've received 120 kaizen reports.

What accounted for this disparity? It did not take long to figure out that their methods were as different as can be. *Company A* was urging people to "submit kaizen," "write kaizen." This upset people, and predictably, they responded by saying things such as, "Too busy," "I can't be bothered," "This is no time for kaizen," etc.

Company B, on the other hand, tried a very different approach. The design department at this company held regular

When the Kaizen System Is Perceived as an End in Itself

monthly meetings, at the beginning of which, kaizen sheets were handed out. Each person then spent about five minutes reviewing his or her work over the past month. Everyone then tried to submit a kaizen report for changes that had resulted in some tangible benefit. Since this was done every month, people were used to it, and it took no longer than five minutes. Sometimes, of course, people were not able to complete the kaizen report in this short time. But more often than not, they at least had time to fill in the problem section (and as we mentioned in the last chapter, once the problem section is filled in, the rest is easy).

The most important point we'd like to make is that *Company B* used kaizen reporting as a tool to review the way people worked, and documentation of implemented improvements came as a by-product of this review process. Therefore, kaizen reporting was

When the Kaizen System Is Perceived as a Means to an End

neither a burden nor a hindrance. The busier people got, the more they realized they had to change the way things got done, and kaizen reporting is a powerful tool to help ensure such changes.

Conversely, *Company A* made kaizen reporting an end in itself. The result was that employees perceived kaizen and work as two completely separate things. For this reason, as soon as things got a little hectic, people felt that there was no time available for improvement activities, because they thought participating in kaizen reporting would interfere with their work.

Either the system becomes an end in itself, or it functions as a tool—a means to improve one's job and working conditions. Understanding a simple fact like this makes a huge difference.

PART

THREE

USING PRACTICAL EXAMPLES TO DRIVE KAIZEN ACTIVITIES

Kaizen starts and ends with examples. But the idea is not to extend the individual improvement ideas horizontally. Instead the idea is to develop and expand in each employee the willingness and ability to implement improvements to his or her work. Using examples to inspire and instruct people is an important part of achieving companywide continuous improvement.

PEOPLE, NOT IDEAS, ARE A COMPANY'S GREATEST ASSETS

13

"If the object is to implement improvements of my own work," someone is sure to ask, "what's the purpose of my making a report and submitting it to the company? After all, isn't what I do in my area irrelevant to other people?" It's a good thing that people are wary about the horizontal deployment of ideas, because it's a throwback to traditional suggestion systems.

WHY HORIZONTAL DEPLOYMENT OF IDEAS DOES NOT WORK

Horizontal deployment is the application of an idea from one department to other departments so that it will be utilized effectively. Managers reason that it's stupid to make similar mistakes and create similar problems at different workplaces in the company. The company can only make progress by extending the

The best solution for a problem in workplace A does not necessarily apply to workplaces B and C.

range of a good idea from one workplace to the whole company. In principle, there is nothing wrong with this theory.

In reality, however, nobody seems to have made much progress with horizontal deployment. There are two reasons for this.

The first reason has to do with the psychological resistance most people feel when it comes to accepting someone else's idea. Even if you know how good an idea is, it is sometimes difficult to accept it with an open heart. We tend to think that somebody else's idea is a "bit of a pain," and for this reason, we avoid doing anything with it.

The second reason is that practically speaking, ideas from another workplace are not much use. It might be a similar workplace, in which a similar job is being done, but the details of the job are never exactly the same. The situation in each section or department differs somewhat, and this being the case, even if an idea has great value at workplace A, it may not be worth much at workplace B.

So, in reality, it's uncommon that an idea deployed horizontally will be accepted. Horizontal deployment is one of those things that sounds great in theory:

- "Let's share our good ideas."
- "Good ideas are the company's assets."

But what people read between the lines is not so encouraging:

Mr. A at workplace A is clever and can come up with lots of good ideas. But people in workplaces B and C are all stupid. Therefore, if they are left on their own, they will never solve any problems. They will surely continue to work in the same stupid way. That's why we have to show them Mr. A's ideas, and they can copy them.

It's understandable that people have such a perception. Horizontal deployment does nothing to develop people or strengthen a company. People are capable of producing improvements continuously, yet when managers press for the horizontal deployment of ideas, it send the message that they have no confidence in the abilities of their workforce.

CULTIVATE THE SOURCE OF GOOD IDEAS

Companies that are good at promoting kaizen activities make the following assumptions: "If Mr. A can think of a kaizen item, then Ms. B and Mr. C should also be able to come up with one. Everyone has this ability. The object of kaizen activities is to extract his ability and use it."

It is management's responsibility, then, to find ways to engage this creative potential that exists within everyone in the workplace.

It is not necessary to make people copy the same small improvement in various places throughout the company. The idea is to create a company in which everyone is encouraged to create their own solutions to the nagging problems that make work difficult, unpleasant, and even unsafe.

One line of thinking holds that ideas are a company's greatest assets, the other is that the real assets are the people who come up with the ideas. In this era of change and diversity, it's impossible to remain competitive unless problems are aggressively solved at each workplace. There's no time to show one idea around and hope people decide to use it.

What is needed is not the horizontal deployment of ideas, but the deployment of the willingness and ability to implement improvements. Implicit in this is the development of skills used for problem awareness, problem analysis, and improvement implementation. When companies build these skills they equip themselves well to cope with changes in the business world.

94

Horizontal Deployment of Improvement Sensibilities

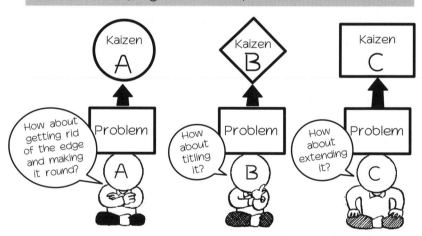

Everyone has the ability to come up with ideas to solve problems; plus, everyone has the ability to continuously implement his or her ideas.

THE PURPOSE OF KAIZEN EXAMPLE BOOKLETS IS TO SHARE IMPROVEMENT POSSIBILITIES

So, if deploying individual ideas horizontally throughout the company is fruitless, why bother with kaizen example booklets? The idea behind these example booklets is to share improvement possibilities. When people in one area of a company see how people in other areas have solved problems, the hope is that the examples will inspire them: "I see. This person came up with an idea to improve her work. What can I do to improve mine?"

The problems of individual work areas are unique; therefore it's best when those who are most familiar with the work of a given area solve the problems of that area.

Sharing Improvement Possibilities

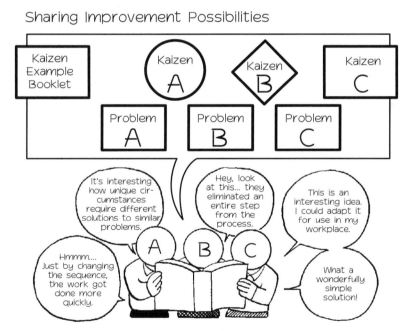

Kaizen examples inspire people to come up with their own creative solutions to the problems of specific work areas.

Kaizen is only possible when the people who are closest to the work are willing and able to implement improvements. Kaizen reports document such willingness and ability, and it is not necessary for their contents to be useful to other work areas within the company. The first purpose is not the horizontal deployment of ideas. The point is to share improvement possibilities and inspire others to demonstrate the willingness and ability to implement their own improvements.

The First Priority Is the Improvement of One's Work

When we say that building the enthusiasm and skills necessary for improvement activities is more important than the horizontal deployment of ideas, we frequently hear the following argument: "It might be true, but if we have a good idea that can be used in other work areas, don't you think we should deploy it horizontally?" When we hear this from a manager, it's a sure bet that the company does not have its priorities straight. The first priority must always be to build the enthusiasm and skills that drive improvement activities. If this is not clarified, employees will be unnecessarily confused. They may think:

- "I have to come up with ideas that will be useful to the company as a whole."
- "I have to do kaizen that pleases other departments."

So, people think about the work of other departments rather than their own work, and eventually they lose their focus.

Of course, it is fine to ask employees to think of something grand—something that contributes to the company as a whole. But the first priority must always be improvement of one's own work. If this is not clarified, a lot of people will neglect the small day-to-day improvements that are the lifeblood of improvement activities. It is always easier to think about other people's work and to make suggestions when you don't have to take any responsibility for them. But this doesn't result in practical solutions to problems. True kaizen does.

The Example Booklet Must Be Simple and Easy to Understand

Since the purpose of the kaizen example book is to inspire people throughout a company to implement improvements, it's best to keep things simple. There is no need to introduce examples of improvements that have resulted in tremendous benefits. Such examples are too specialized for kaizen promotion. It's unlikely that people in other departments will understand them, and therefore they will not read them. The only happy person will be the one with whom the idea originated.

Furthermore, examples of such upper-grade implementations will intimidate people and dampen their enthusiasm for improvement activities. That's why examples of implemented improvements should be simple and comprehensible. Then a lot

97

of people will read them and think, "If this is good enough, then I can do it too, no problem. In fact, what if I were to..." Don't underestimate the power of easily understood examples to motivate people to implement their own improvements.

The purpose of kaizen activities is to direct employees' awareness towards improvement opportunities. Compared to innovation, kaizen is subtle and modest. Therefore, these small examples of implemented improvements must be cherished and carefully evaluated. To keep people focused on small, implemented improvements, it helps if companies use example booklets and other promotional materials to communicate the following message: "Small improvements that you make to your work every day make a *big* difference in the long run."

INNOVATION, KAIZEN,

AND SMALL

GROUP ACTIVITIES

In our experience, it's highly unusual to see front-line employees repeatedly implement improvements that yield rewards of tens of thousands of yen (upwards of about $70). This is because such large-scale improvements and innovations are the responsibility of specialists and executives. If front-line employees could consistently implement such high-level improvements and innovations, there would be no need to employ (and pay for) highly trained experts.

Of course, we are all human. Specialists and executives are not gods. They make mistakes and miss things. And front-line employees occasionally come up with extraordinary ideas, although rewards in excess of ¥10,000 ($70) account for less than one percent of all rewards. In companies that have successfully activated kaizen systems, rewards of ¥1,000 ($7) account for 90 to 95 percent of all rewards. This data also shows that these companies attach great importance to small improvements whose rewards are between ¥500 ($3.50) and ¥1,000 ($7).

Don't Expect Everyone to Hit a Home Run

A manager who expects employees to always implement large-scale improvements under the kaizen system is like a baseball coach who tells every player to hit a home run. Logically, if everyone hits a homer, you will win every game very easily. But it doesn't happen in real life, and teams led by such coaches will not win many games.

A realistic coach tells the players "just get a hit or a walk." He or she will not expect all the players to hit home runs, but will coach the best players to produce a few.

Similarly, a company manager should never ask or expect the average employee to come up with innovative ideas. If this what managers expect, they are likely to be disappointed, because employees will constantly "strike out." In realistic management,

Kaizen Means Encouraging Attainable Results from Everyone

innovation is the responsibility of managers, small workplace improvements are the responsibility of the average employee. So, in promoting kaizen activities, it's not wise to ask or appeal for

- big benefits
- high-level improvements
- ideas that can be deployed throughout the company

The focus instead needs to be on small workplace improvements, and companies should emphasize this point through their example booklets and kaizen promotional materials.

KAIZEN CAN'T THRIVE WITHOUT INNOVATION

If you're wondering about the relationship between kaizen and innovation, you're in good company. "You repeatedly emphasize that small workplace improvements are the key to success," many say, "but will this solve our more substantive problems? We can't stay competitive just by making minor improvements. We need more radical changes. We need innovation."

What's needed is clarification of the relationship between kaizen and innovation.

Innovation Is a Bulldozer

Innovation is like using a bulldozer to cut a path through the jungle. New business development and new product development require huge investment, high risk, and special abilities. Therefore, innovation is not something that anybody can handle. Only people with the proper authority and position within the company have sufficient responsibility to tackle it.

Improvement activities, on the other hand, provide a means of leveling the path cut by the bulldozer and paving it to turn it into a smooth road. Thus, unless the bulldozer of innovation cuts the path, the kaizen "road crews" won't be able to do anything.

In other words, companies that rest on their laurels—companies in which there is no management innovation for the future—do not need kaizen. The employees will simply have to carry on with their work just as they always have. A company setting up a kaizen system, providing rewards, and appealing seriously for small workplace improvements is most certainly engaging in innovation simultaneously.

There is nothing more wasteful than trying to activate a kaizen system in a company that is not engaged in innovation. If the bulldozer stays still, there will be no path on which to pave a road. Trying to clear a path with a pick and shovel will not do when your competitors are using a bulldozer.

It is said that you cannot compensate for strategic errors with stratagems. Similarly, you cannot compensate for a shortage of innovations with kaizen activities.

Let's just say for the sake of discussion that the innovative efforts of a company president create a benefit of ¥10,000 ($70) and that small workplace improvements implemented by front-line workers create a benefit of ¥100 ($.70). This means that even if 100 employees wholeheartedly pursue improvement activities, a strategic mistake by the company owner is capable of

---

Kaizen Can't Thrive without Innovation

Grind! Clunk! Groan! Vroom!

Vroom!

Now I can smooth the path.

wiping out whatever beneficial effects have accumulated. This is why we say that kaizen cannot thrive without innovation.

An Era in Which Small Improvements Make a Big Difference

Although it's not possible for companies to survive without innovation, innovation alone will not ensure success. If we make an analogy using weapons of war, then advanced weapons such as missiles and jet fighters, which have tremendous destructive power, represent innovation.

But military power also depends greatly upon infantry forces. What chance do infantry soldiers equipped with carbine rifles have against opposing forces equipped with automatic weapons and machine guns? To upgrade soldiers' weapons from carbines to automatic rifles is a small improvement compared to developing new types of missiles and aircraft. Yet without making such a "small" improvement, it's entirely likely that the military advantage gained by using sophisticated weapons will be offset by ill-equipped infantry forces. Similarly, companies simply can't continue to compete effectively if employees are not upgrading their capabilities by participating in kaizen activities.

Innovation will always create opportunities for new work and improvements to that work, and it's management's job to make sure that this kind of situation exists. In fact, in companies that aggressively tackle innovation, no matter how hard employees work to implement small improvements, there will never be a shortage of opportunities to implement additional ones. Even before people have leveled and paved the last path, the bulldozer of innovation is already clearing another path!

Employees may grumble a bit, but just on the surface. In reality, they are likely to be pleased, for two basic reasons. First, they are pleased that they get the chance to learn and grow as they implement new improvements. Second, in these increasingly uncertain and competitive times, their efforts ensure the success of their employer, thus creating greater job security.

Only through constant kaizen activity does a company build such a strong constitution. Small improvements every day *can* make a big difference.

HOW KAIZEN RELATES TO SMALL GROUP ACTIVITIES

Companies with QC circles and small group activities have to integrate them with the kaizen reporting system. Employees may become confused if a company promotes both types of activity separately, and they will surely complain if they have to do QC and then kaizen on top of that. What sort of action must be taken to overcome this situation?

Individuals Solve Small Problems; Small Groups Tackle Big Problems

In the workplace, there are some problems as big as a bull and others as small as a chicken. It would be absurd for a group of people to run around chasing a chicken with huge carving knives in their hands, trying to kill it. On the other hand, it would be unwise to try to subdue an overexcited bull with your bare hands. In other words,

- QC circles and other types of small group activities are for analyzing and solving complicated problems.
- Individuals solve minor problems on the spot and document their efforts in kaizen reports.

What's the purpose of collecting data or creating detailed, colorful charts to communicate something that's easily understood? There is no need to drag in a group to discuss something that can be done by an individual. This is something we often see in circle activities that have been formalized for the sake of presentation. If employees are still at the learning stage, it's okay. But companies serious about improvement don't tolerate it indefinitely.

Small Group Activities Are a Safeguard Against Superficial Kaizen

The power of the kaizen system is derived from the speed with which decisions, implementations, and evaluations take place. The system empowers every employee to take immediate steps toward improvement—to do whatever is possible and within his or her means. This is as it should be if companies are to keep up with ever-changing markets.

Managers and executives who have a lot on the ball continuously review the needs and wants of customers, redirecting corporate activities as necessary. The kaizen system contributes toward a flexible business that can respond quickly to whatever changes are necessary in order to keep old customers and acquire new ones.

There is a catch, however. Since a main feature of the kaizen system is speed, it is not uncommon for companies, in their haste to implement improvements, to end up making problems worse or creating new ones. True kaizen, of course, seeks countermeasures that address the root causes of problems. But if training and education are insufficient, improvement activities become shallow and without much substance.

And then there are complex problems that one person simply cannot solve without the help of others. In any case, learning about QC techniques within small groups is a safeguard against creating countermeasures that do not adequately address root causes.

When companies integrate kaizen reporting and QC circles, they greatly increase the chances of achieving the two main objectives of the kaizen system:

- continuous implementation of improvements
- development of employees' problem solving and implementation skills

Small group activities and kaizen reporting have in common the goal of improving work. The difference is the means and tools used to achieve this end, and it's best to be sure that you are using the right tool for the right job.

THE PROMOTION OF KAIZEN ACTIVITIES BEGINS AND ENDS WITH PRACTICAL EXAMPLES

There are a lot of companies whose kaizen activities are rather dull, in spite of the efforts made to promote them. To be sure, promotion committees spend a great deal of time and money planning events and producing manuals, example booklets, and other promotional materials. Nevertheless, sad to say, most of these efforts are not carefully directed, and there are many cases where these diligent efforts bring about adverse effects instead of the intended benefits.

PRACTICAL EXAMPLES ARE THE BEST TEXTBOOK

We recommend that companies stick to the following theme when creating example booklets and other promotional materials: small workplace improvements. Everyone is capable of understanding examples that reflect this theme, and the more comprehensible the examples, the more employees will become involved in improvement activities. Very simple kaizen examples can give a lot of confidence to employees, and develop the willingness to participate. Also, easily understood examples help people learn the basic principles of kaizen—methods of problem analysis, problem solving, and implementation.

When companies produce example booklets or posters, they often highlight and introduce only "superior" kaizen, but this is a mistake. If the purpose is to appeal to people to implement small workplace improvements, then it's necessary to spotlight such improvements.

Spotlighting innovative improvements is appropriate in promoting traditional suggestion systems, in which the first

LET'S Implement improvements

—— Example presentation corner

For those who are having a hard time coming up with small workplace improvements, here are 3 examples to inspire you.

No. 1 Making a stand for capillary tubes used for red blood cell inspection

For red blood cell inspection, blood is placed in capillary tubes that contain dyes, then the tubes are shaken to mix the contents together. Before the improvement we used to do the mixing one capillary tube at a time. But when more than two tubes needed to be mixed, this was a waste of time. The stand we created helps us save time by mixing the contents of many tubes at the same time. We numbered the grooves to avoid confusion

(Before)

Capillary tube

Good mixing

(After)

Polystyrene holder

spring issue

NEWS

Summer Edition 1990

Sony Proposal Recognition Program

Source: Sony

priority is obtaining big effects and giving big rewards. But if the goal is to develop human resources, then spotlighting innovative improvements is likely to alienate and intimidate a lot of people, thus thwarting activation of the kaizen system. People learn by doing. But if they cannot be persuaded to participate in improvement implementation, they won't develop new skills.

Participation goes up when examples highlight simple workplace improvements in a way that's simple to understand. The figure on the opposite page shows such an example.

We don't mean to suggest that it's unreasonable to honor originators of superior kaizen in the company newsletter. But to only do so is unfair. Generally speaking, high-level improvements are implemented by people who possess special qualifications and greater responsibilities within the company. This is why the promotion committee should give first priority to examples that show well-conceived and simple solutions to problems more typically faced by the average employee.

109

PRACTICAL EXAMPLES ARE AN INVALUABLE TREASURE

What is the strength of kaizen? It is teaching about things that actually exist. We are not talking about abstract theories. We are talking about the countless teaching opportunities that exist within a company. Every kaizen report, in fact, is a potential teaching tool.

Top managers may find meaning in long reports and tables of data. But the people on the shop floor—the people whose participation determines the success or failure of a kaizen system—will most likely not even look at such things. It's as if they are allergic to abstract words and dull data.

Practical examples, however, will capture people's attention. Nothing motivates people better than seeing examples of simple workplace improvements implemented by their colleagues. In order to use these wonderful resources most effectively, we recommend, as the examples in this chapter show, that they be arranged in a way that's easy to understand, and that they be distributed to everyone and displayed on the walls. Of course, it is not unacceptable to present examples of improvements implemented at other companies, but this is like carrying coals to Newcastle. Just as Newcastle possesses an abundant source of coal, most companies possess a rich source of examples from which people can learn the basic principles of kaizen.

Fill the Instruction Manual with "Live" Kaizen

The next page shows part of a kaizen teian instruction manual. It shows how to fill in the form, using a real improvement example. What if the manual did not use an example? Nobody would have bothered to take the time to read it through, because it would have been too dull and boring. If there is a simple example, it will draw people's attention and stir their interest. Without consciously trying, they will learn about the rules and the form.

We have seen a lot of kaizen instruction manuals produced by various companies, and they are often very abstract, providing little more than surface knowledge. Although these manuals have fine-sounding titles such as, "The Meaning of Kaizen Teian," "How to Create Ideas," "Steps to Kaizen," etc., it is easy to see that these are just transcriptions or bits and pieces of other books.

Nobody will read them. They cannot even be used for reference. Instead of using these irrelevant materials, companies should use examples of improvements that have been implemented by their own employees. Using familiar examples is the best way to help people truly understand what kaizen really is.

Make Posters with Examples on Them

It is best to create example booklets by using easily understood and interesting examples. But you do not need a booklet at

Source: Shintsu Chemical Co.

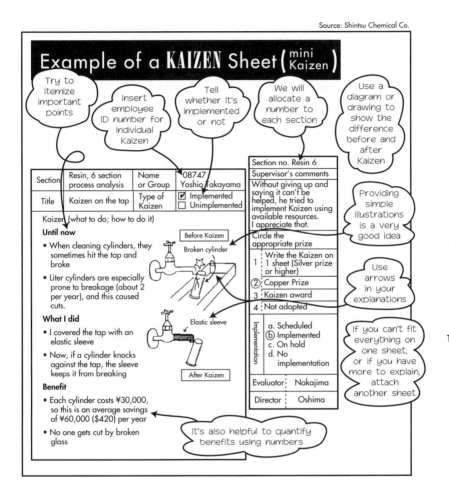

111

the beginning. Rather than that, it might be better to introduce a few examples every month using posters or internal newsletters. This relieves the pressure on those promoting improvement activities. Like television commercials, which provide information continuously in segments, posters can be extremely effective tools for promotion.

The reproductions of the posters on pages 112 and 113 show a target set for kaizen activities combined with an introduction of some examples. What if the posters only communicated the

target? No one would stop and look at them, and if they did, they might feel pressured and a bit disgusted. On the other hand, when the target is presented with an interesting example, even if people turn away from the numbers, they may be interested enough to look at the example.

Because the examples come from their colleagues, people are interested, and they feel familiar with the situation. People might make comments like the following:

- "I see that improvement was so and so's idea..."
- "Yes, that's a big improvement."
- "There might be another way to get the same result."
- "It might be even better if we did this..."
- "I can apply this idea in my work; it's given me a clue..."

Subsequent improvements follow naturally.

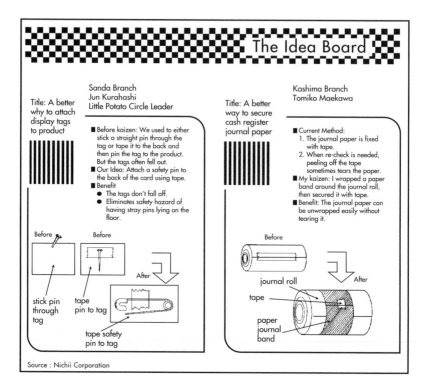

Posters like the ones shown above that include examples are much better than posters that only emphasize improvement targets. You can change the example part every month, and you can always provide a new piece of information or a new topic. This will not only avoid monotony, but also attract further interest. People will look forward to seeing whose example will be featured next. Perhaps they will even consciously attempt to implement an improvement worthy of being featured.

In addition, since the target will not change throughout the year, the posters will remind people continuously of the company's improvement goals. This is an extremely efficient method of promotion.

At the end of the year, the posters can be reduced in size, and voila! you have a book of examples like the ones shown on pages

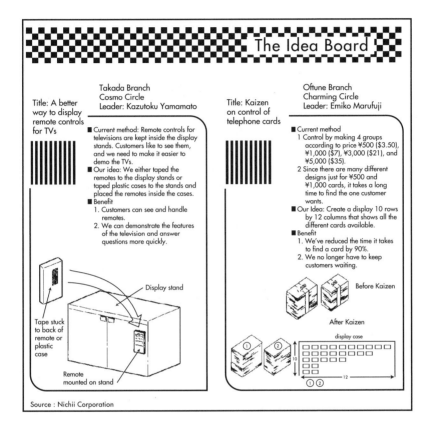

The Idea Board

Title: A better way to display remote controls for TVs

Takada Branch
Cosmo Circle
Leader: Kazutoku Yamamato

■ Current method: Remote controls for televisions are kept inside the display stands. Customers like to see them, and we need to make it easier to demo the TVs.
■ Our idea: We either taped the remotes to the display stands or taped plastic cases to the stands and placed the remotes inside the cases.
■ Benefit
1. Customers can see and handle remotes.
2. We can demonstrate the features of the television and answer questions more quickly.

Display stand

Tape stuck to back of remote or plastic case

Remote mounted on stand

Title: Kaizen on control of telephone cards

Oftune Branch
Charming Circle
Leader: Emiko Marufuji

■ Current method
1 Control by making 4 groups according to price ¥500 ($3.50), ¥1,000 ($7), ¥3,000 ($21), and ¥5,000 ($35).
2 Since there are many different designs just for ¥500 and ¥1,000 cards, it takes a long time to find the one customer wants.
■ Our Idea: Create a display 10 rows by 12 columns that shows all the different cards available.
■ Benefit
1. We've reduced the time it takes to find a card by 90%.
2. We no longer have to keep customers waiting.

Before Kaizen

After Kaizen

display case

Source : Nichii Corporation

116 through 119. It doesn't matter that people have seen these examples before. Compiled into a booklet, they offer new opportunities for learning and inspiration. Even if people have seen the examples before, they examine them with a fresh point of view. The booklet serves as a record of people's improvement efforts. A huge effect can be achieved with just a minimal effort on the part of the people in charge, and this is by far the most efficient of all the methods of management and promotion.

Promoters Must Dig Out Examples

In order to introduce examples on a continuous basis, it is efficient to use internal newsletters. Some companies even print

Inageya's Kaizen Booklet

Putting casters on a stand for umbrella covers

No. 10

Current situation
Whenever it starts raining, one of the sales assistants has to bring an umbrella cover stand to the front from a back room.

Problem
The scale weights over 15kg, so it's very heavy and difficult to carry.

Improvement
We put 2 casters on the stands at a cost of ¥270 each.
Total cost:¥540
(about $3.75)

It's so easy

Benefit
Nice and dry

Telling hot from cold

Current situation
The color of the hoses leading from both the hot and cold water taps is blue.

Problem
It's hard to tell hot from cold.

Improvement
We attached a red hose to the hot water tap and a blue hose to the cold water tap.

Hot   Cold

Red

Blue

Benefit
Even if the hoses get tangled up, it's still possible to tell which is for hot water and which is for cold water.

Storing and ordering dispatch forms

No. 8

Current situation
The forms are kept below the service counter as the following picture shows.

Service Counter

Forms

acrylic partition

Problem
We sometimes run out of forms, because there is no standard for re-ordering them.

Improvement
We decided that the two people in charge of the service counter, a branch manager and a customer service representative, should be in charge of ordering forms. To ensure that they are ordered at the right time, we created a cardboard case for the forms. The inside of the case is painted red up to a height of 30 sheets. As soon as the person attending to the service counter sees red, he or she orders more forms.

Benefit
1. We no longer forget to order more forms.
2. Even those not in charge can see when new forms need to be ordered.

Painted red.

Source: Inageya

newsletters dedicated solely to improvement news. In any case, we recommend that the people in charge always dig out and select examples by themselves.

People in charge of improvement activities at big companies sometimes brag rather arrogantly that since only superior kaizen reaches their headquarters, they don't know what they have in terms of simple kaizen. This is not good. The main thrust of kaizen activities is small improvements, and if you are not aware of such efforts, then you cannot successfully promote a kaizen system. Digging out examples is the best way to find out what is happening at the forefront of improvement activities.

In Chapter 12 we discussed how the kaizen system provides a positive tool for fact-based evaluations that focus on strengths rather than weaknesses. The number of improvements that people implement, then, is a barometer of supervisors' abilities to coach and advise; and as their skills increase, so do the numbers of implemented improvements. So it's likely there will be lots of simple examples from which promoters may choose. Therefore, the best barometer of the ability and commitment of kaizen promoters is the extent to which they are able to find and call attention to easy and interesting examples.

A Form for Connecting Train Information

Osaka Conductor
Ikuo Kawabata

★ Current situation / problem
— Passengers always ask me about connecting trains, and I used to just say that such and such a train was leaving from platform X.
★ Idea
— I came up with the idea of creating a form that I could hand out to passengers.
★ Kaizen implementation

This is easy

Connecting Information

Train no. ___ will arrive at ___ . After___ minutes, train no. ___will leave from platform ___.
Change trains at ___ station. There will be a train stopping at ___ and ___ . You will arrive at your destination at ___ . Thank you for riding with us!

Making sure that

★ Current situation/problem
— When leaving the office in the evenings we can't remember to take off our shoes in order
★ Idea
— So that we can see if the window is locked, we put a strip of phosphorescent tape on the part of the lock that show through the window when it's locked.
★ Kaizen Implementation

Phosphorescent tape

Cool. It's closed

★ Benefit
— Customers receiv accurate informa

Benefit
— It saves time. You can see from outside whether the windows are locked and don't have to go back in every time and take off your shoes to check

Making a Box to Keep Keys Organized

Aioi Denryoku of Koji Aota Company

▶ What made you think about this?
—All the keys were kept in a small box, and it was ha to find the right key when we needed it.
▶ What did you do?
— We made a box that included a map to show what each key was for and where it should go.
▶ What happened?
— We don't have to search for keys anymore and since they are arranged according to location, it's easy to ...erstand.

tangled

Key box

Map of locations

Map of locations

▶ Comments:
This is especially useful at times of accidents.

▶ Idea
Put the cord through the shaft of the rotating table and attach a rubber band so that it only rotates halfway

It will be easier to use

Rubber band
Cord

▶ Benefit
It's easy to handle and the cords don't get tangled.

Source: JR Nishi Nippon

Choose Examples That Demonstrate Company Improvement Goals

The examples shown on pages 118 and 119 come from a company that has switched from a traditional suggestion system to a kaizen reporting system. They have achieved brilliant results in a short time. Every one of the examples introduced is simple and small, but they are all improvements that the employees have appreciated and taken to heart.

Whenever we check our work, we realize that we get into arguments, have a hard time, or waste our time because of surprisingly petty things. In this company, kaizen activities were developed with the idea that such petty inconveniences should be eliminated one by one. Accordingly, kaizen promoters chose examples showing improvement activities related to this goal. Doing so was a key to their success.

Companies that manage improvement activity promotion poorly often show great disparity between promotional policy and example presentation.

The Example Booklet Shows the Accumulated Wisdom of the Employees

We recommend that at the beginning, companies focus on presenting and making a booklet of comprehensible, simple, familiar and small examples that relate to the established improvement goals. The accumulation of example booklets represents the fundamental power of the company and its employees. The example booklets also prove that the company encourages improvements, and that people have implemented improvements and accumulated know-how.

It doesn't matter how many books written by reputable experts you buy. Such books contain only knowledge, not wisdom. But "in-house" experts—i.e., a company's employees—write the example booklets. Therefore, these booklets contain a great deal of wisdom. They address problems either with which everyone is familiar, or in which everyone has some sort of interest as a matter of simple company pride. Once a company has accumulated lots of examples, there are numerous ways to organize them for teaching and promotional purposes. The preparation of such materials crystallizes the wisdom of the workforce. It's a good idea to include a postscript in example booklets similar to the one shown at the end of this chapter.

THE EXPERIENCE OF IMPLEMENTING SMALL IMPROVEMENTS IS THE RUNWAY TO GREATER IMPROVEMENTS

Because we constantly urge companies to keep things simple at the beginning stages of improvement activities, we are frequently asked how long it is necessary to maintain activities at this level.

If a kaizen system is regarded as a significant corporate activity then it is reasonable to expect that it will eventually produce benefits relevant to the investment. From this point of view, it is unacceptable that people continue to implement only ultra-simple improvements indefinitely. But it is also important not to confuse the start with the final goal.

Figuratively speaking, companies need a long enough runway to get the kaizen reporting system off the ground. In order to do this, managers and supervisors must

1. build enthusiasm for improvement activities
2. habituate people to improvement implementation

It is for this reason that even very simple improvements should be accepted with gratitude and great enthusiasm. This phase is the runway to lasting continuous improvement. If, as we stated earlier, companies don't economize when it comes to priming the improvement pump, this runway will be precisely as long as it needs to be.

121

Why? No greater sense of achievement exists than implementing your own improvements and seeing the benefits confirmed in your daily work. Once people have the experience of implementing improvements that make their work easier, they will naturally strive for greater achievements. Because humans possess a natural desire for improvement, it's unlikely that conscientious efforts to activate a kaizen reporting system will get stuck in the startup phase.

In this early phase, improvements are likely to address symptoms of problems, but eventually an evolution takes place. People begin to create countermeasures that address root causes, and this leads to greater, more significant improvements. Of course, it is necessary to provide guidance and training so that people understand what real improvement is and the kinds of improvements that are expected. It is especially important to always clarify targets that a company expects its employees to reach.

DISCOVER
YOUR OWN **KAIZEN** Principles and Idea Rules

What do you think of the examples we have shown you?

All the examples introduced here are small workplace improvements. They didn't result in big profits or outstanding achievements for the company. However, they do represent ways that people have solved problems and overcome hardships creatively. Some of the ideas, in fact, are quite ingenious.

Regardless of the type and size of the improvement, you can find in each one of these examples the principles of implementing kaizen and methods for generating ideas. For example:

- By visualizing the problem and defining it, you get a better understanding of the present situation and create counter-measures to solve problems.
- By adding or subtracting something, you sometimes make the work easier and more efficient.
- By changing procedures and the order of operations, you can sometimes create a situation in which work is done in parallel, which is quicker than before.

Please read the book again and as you do so ask yourself which method or principle is demonstrated in each example. Then you will be able to find your own method of implementing improvements of your own work. It may also give you some ideas for tackling even bigger kaizen.

PART

F

O

U

R

KAIZEN TEIAN
EXAMPLES

The following stories are more than just testimonials to the positive effects of kaizen teian activities. They also show the process by which an improvement-oriented sensibility emerges, as well as the development of the skills and confidence that make it possible to follow through on improvement ideas until they are implemented.

Every year the Japan Human Relations Association (JHRA) holds public meetings in Tokyo, Osaka, and Nagoya. The examples that follow were selected from presentations made at these meetings and have been published previously in JHRA's magazine, *Ingenuity and*

Invention. The companies represented in the examples are

FUJICOLOR SERVICES CO. LTD.

•

OSAKA GAS LTD.

•

THE PACK

•

NISSAN MOTORS

•

MIZUNO

•

MEIJI DAIRY PRODUCTS

KAIZEN ACTIVITIES THAT FOCUS ON CONVENIENCE TO COLLEAGUES AND CUSTOMERS

---

*by Yuko Ishida
of Fujicolor Services Co. Ltd.*

Fujicolor Services has been in business for close to 50 years, providing film and photo-related products to portrait studios, movie production companies, advertising agencies, small film processors, exhibition display companies, professional photographers, and photo shops.

I work in Fujicolor's Nagoya sales office, and I'm responsible for purchasing, issuing invoices, preparing monthly sales reports, and keeping track of all documents.

When I first joined the company in 1985, I was aware of the kaizen system but was completely indifferent to it. I was busy and didn't want to be bothered. I recognize now that I was intimidated. I thought that kaizen was difficult and also that I'd be embarrassed if I couldn't think of really good ideas. During my first four years at the company, I observed that the salespeople I worked with were also indifferent to the kaizen system.

But then one day, another woman in the department showed me reports of some of the improvement proposals she had implemented. She had come up with lots of wonderful ideas. What struck me was that they were all so simple. Kaizen wasn't complicated at all! It gave me confidence that I could come up with my own ideas.

Using her ideas for inspiration, I began thinking of ways I might make my work easier. Many of my first suggestions, in fact, were variations of the proposals that had inspired me. I was worried about this, but it turned out to be okay. Since then, I've come up with lots of ideas of my own, and I'd like to share some of them with you.

A DIRECTORY FOR FREQUENTLY USED FAX NUMBERS

My work space is near the sales department's fax machine. Although all my colleagues had their own directories of commonly called numbers, they got into the habit of asking me for the right number when they came to send a fax. Can you imagine how annoying this was?

I had an insight one day that I could use our photocopying machine to reduce the size of the fax directory. Then I laminated this minidirectory and taped it to the machine in a conspicuous place. Now I'm happy because I don't get interrupted as much, and my colleagues are happy because I've made it easier for them to send a fax.

INSTRUCTION MANUAL FOR INPUTTING NEW CUSTOMER DATA

Whenever we start doing business with a new customer, we have to input data into our computer. Often this has to be done immediately to avoid delay in processing a new order. Although inputting the data is a simple task, I was the only one who knew how to do it, which meant that whenever we started dealing with a new customer, I would have to drop whatever I was doing.

My solution to this problem was to create a short, step-by-step manual that showed others how to input this important data. I then laminated it and attached it to the computer. Now, anyone can input data, which makes my work easier and eliminates the possibility that new customers might be inconvenienced.

CUTTING THE COST AND IMPROVING THE DISTRIBUTION OF MINI PHOTO ALBUMS

One of the products we offer to our customers is a miniature photo album, and it's my responsibility to order them from our supplier. One month, the management at Fujicolor was promoting a cost-reduction campaign, and I began thinking about ways I might contribute.

A short while later, when it was time to reorder mini albums from our regular supplier—*Company A*—I remembered that we had received a cheaper quote from another supplier—*Company B*—and thought we might buy from them and save money. I told my supervisor my idea, but he rejected it. He thought that the quality of *Company B's* album was inferior to *Company A's*.

Although I was turned down, I wasn't discouraged. I showed *Company A's* album to a representative of *Company B* and asked if they could make something similar at the price they had quoted. They agreed to do it, and the subsequent cost savings came to ¥25,000 ($175) per month–or ¥300,000 ($2,100) per year.

One day, after we had started stocking mini albums from *Company B*, I had reason to visit our warehouse. There I saw stacks and stacks of the albums and people working very hard to fulfill orders. I had never realized before what an enormous job it was to sort and deliver these albums.

After I left the warehouse, I called my representative at *Company B* and asked if they would deliver albums directly to our customers. At first, they rejected the idea, but when I showed them that it would not increase their transportation costs, they agreed. (See the illustration on pages 130 and 131.)

Before Kaizen

SUPPLIER

order

Nagoya office

delivery

Sorting and delivering mini albums is a huge task

A
B
C
D
E
F
G
H
I

330
Customers

KAIZEN AWARENESS

When I do kaizen, I often start by putting myself in another person's shoes. This gets me thinking about ways that I might make my colleagues' work, as well as my own, easier.

As I walk around the office, I look for clues—problems and opportunities for improvement—and do what I can to make appropriate changes. When I take calls from customers I listen carefully to their problems and complaints and also try to address those in my kaizen efforts.

I've found that it's helpful to make a note of problems and improvement opportunities as they occur to me, and that's why I carry my kaizen memo pad with me all the time. It helps me keep track of problems to solve, which I later submit as kaizen.

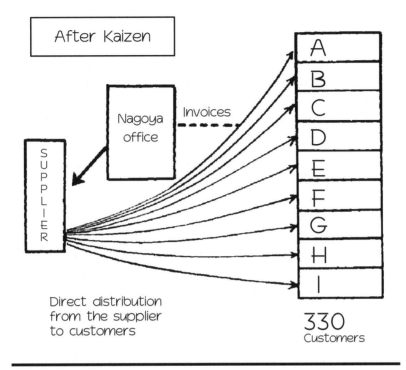

After Kaizen

Nagoya office

Invoices

SUPPLIER

A
B
C
D
E
F
G
H
I

Direct distribution
from the supplier
to customers

330
Customers

When I first started doing kaizen in earnest, I motivated myself by writing out a list:

1. Prepare a memo every morning at my desk.
2. Implement 50 improvements per month.
3. Be aware of "the competition."
4. Organize the workplace and keep it tidy.
5. Do kaizen to make everyone's work easier.
6. Be conscious of kaizen at work throughout the whole day.

When I'm in a slump, I find it helpful to do the following things:

- Listen very carefully to others' problems for kaizen ideas.

- Review my previous kaizen reports for refinements I might make.
- Refer to the reports of others available in the kaizen promotion office.
- Try to think of solutions to problems that come up in QC group discussions.
- Ask my supervisor for help.
- Walk around other areas (especially the warehouse) to look for things that need to be improved.
- Examine kaizen leaflets from other companies to identify good ideas that I can apply to my own work.

By doing these things to raise my awareness, I'm proud to report that I became the top kaizen submitter in my company. My efforts have been acknowledged in our company's newsletter, and I've been praised frequently at monthly meetings. Currently, I've set a target of 60 kaizen per month for the second half of the year, and thanks to the encouragement of my supervisors, I'm confident I'll be able to reach it.

It's nice, of course, to be lavished with attention; and I certainly appreciate the rewards I receive—especially before payday! But what's been best for me, I think, has been learning that when I want to accomplish something, I can.

UPPER-GRADE IMPROVEMENT TO A BOG COMPRESSOR

by Chikara Kairiku
of Osaka Gas Ltd.

Osaka Gas serves five million people in the Kinki region of Japan. We liquefy natural gas collected in Indonesia and bring it to our plants in tankers. In the plants we process the gas continuously, 24 hours a day.

My department deals mainly with the maintenance of production equipment in all the plants. One of our most important pieces of equipment is a BOG compressor, which takes its name from the fact that it boils off gas. I'll explain more about this shortly. For now, suffice it to say that we were having all sorts of problems with this machine.

Liquefied natural gas (LNG) is stored in tanks at the extremely low temperature of -160 degrees Celsius. Due to the great difference in temperature inside the tank and outside, the LNG is constantly evaporating, and it's necessary to eliminate vapor in the tank before the LNG can be processed for use by our customers. That's what the BOG compressor does.

BOG Compressor, cross-section

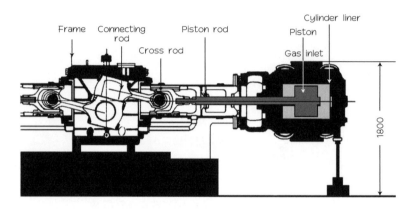

The BOG compressor is a fairly big machine—about 7 meters wide and 2 meters high. Basically, it consists of a piston and a cylinder. It sucks gas through the inlet at the top and then blows it out the bottom. The piston moves from left to right; the motor lies in the center. It's a sophisticated piece of equipment, but drawn more simply and stood on end, it's just like a bicycle pump.

The piston weighs 300 kilograms, and it moves at the tremendously high speed of about 600 strokes per minute. With most normal compressors, you can prevent wear by inserting lubricating grease between the cylinder and the piston. But the BOG compressor handles very low-temperature gas, and it's not possible to use grease; it would freeze. Instead, the BOG compressor uses rider rings to maintain the gap between the surfaces of the piston and cylinder, thus keeping them from rubbing together.

The problem, however, is that the rider rings have a finite life. After a certain number of operational hours, the rings break down and the piston and cylinder come into direct contact. Trying to predict the degree of wear proved to be difficult. If the

Drawn simply and stood on end, the BOG compressor is not unlike a bicycle pump.

Structure of Compressor

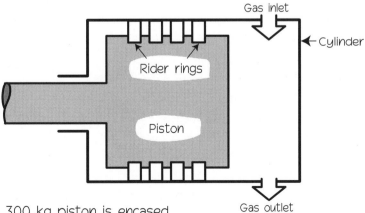

300 kg piston is encased inside cylinder.
Rider rings separate metal surfaces.

rings wore out more quickly than we predicted and the piston and cylinder came into contact, the necessary repairs cost us ¥5 to ¥6 million (about $35,000 to $42,000)! If, on the other hand, we discarded a ring too soon, we prevented costly repairs; but this was still wasteful. I wondered what to do about this situation.

I have formed the habit of filling my head with information from lots of different sources: specialized technical magazines, manufacturer's specifications, catalogs, reports, handwritten memos to myself after meetings with colleagues, etc. According to a book I once read on leadership, good ideas often come at unexpected times from unexpected places. Sure enough, one day, when I was leafing through a stack of "techno cards" that showed different kinds of equipment, one of the cards—unrelated to the BOG compressor—talked about "measuring the gap."

We had been so obsessed with restrictions such as high pressure, low temperature, and high speed that we had completely overlooked this possibility. If the rider rings were wearing

away, then the gap between the piston and the cylinder would grow smaller. So all we had to do was find a reliable way to measure this gap and get immediate feedback. Then we'd know precisely when the rider rings needed to be changed.

We thought of two similar ways to measure the gap, both of which made use of a sensor and an eddy current.[*] One method placed the sensor within the piston; the other method placed it against the outside surface of the cylinder. Although initial experiments on a model were very satisfactory, we discovered some problems that ultimately made the idea unfeasible:

137

- We couldn't find a battery that could supply power to the sensor continuously over its one-year life span.
- The low temperature impaired the efficiency of the sensor.
- We couldn't stop the machine immediately.

Frustrated, I wanted to forget about this problem for a while, so I sought a diversion. I picked up a model car that I keep in my office and absently rolled it along the top of my desk, enjoying

---

[*]An electrical current which is generated (and dissipated) in a conductive material in the presence of an electromagnetic field.

1 mm grove
← Cylinder
Beam emitted
Beam received
Piston
Optical fiber
← Rider ring

Optical Fiber Measuring Device

Theoretically, this sensor should detect any downward movement of the piston as the rider rings degrade.

the quiet sound of the rubber tires against the hard surface. It was then I remembered that many real cars have an indicator light that tells the driver when the tire treads have worn down.

This helped me reframe my thought process. Measuring the gap was one way to know when the rider rings had deteriorated. What happens to the piston, I asked myself, when the ring starts to deteriorate? It moves down, of course. I figured there had to be some way to detect this movement.

We came up with the idea of putting one-millimeter grooves in the piston head and using an optical fiber to detect any downward movement that might occur. We were really excited about this idea, but in practice, it didn't work; machine vibration made it impossible to get an accurate measurement.

Determined to find a workable solution, I came up with the idea for a Teflon-coated wear sensor. The concept was simple: When the rider rings wore down, the piston would make contact with the Teflon, activating a current in hair-thin copper wires

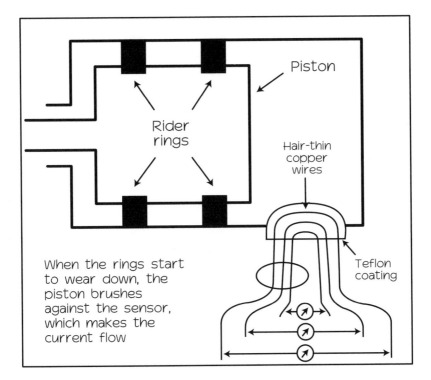

Piston

Rider
rings

Hair-thin
copper
wires

Teflon
coating

When the rings start
to wear down, the
piston brushes
against the sensor,
which makes the
current flow

139

leading to and from the sensor. It was a great idea in theory. But it probably won't surprise you to learn that the thought of introducing a live wire anywhere near a highly explosive substance strikes terror into the hearts of us natural gas engineers!

Although the idea proved impractical, it did serve as a bridge to the next idea: How about using an optical fiber instead of an electric current?

Now when the rider rings wore down and the piston made contact with the sensor, it would cut off the flow of light through the optical fiber, giving us the immediate feedback we were seeking. And it worked!

Since we've implemented this idea, achieving an important maintenance standard for a valuable piece of equipment, we've reduced maintenance costs by ¥1.45 million ($10,150) per year and also expect income from sales of our technology to other

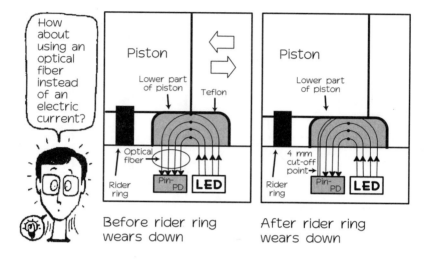

Before rider ring
wears down

After rider ring
wears down

companies. We have received three patents, and our efforts were reported in three separate newspaper articles and two magazine articles.

There are several different factors involved in creating lasting improvements. When they are all "in sync," you can accomplish great things. I will keep making kaizen; I believe in this process.

SMALL GROUP ACTIVITIES HELP BREAK THROUGH PROBLEM SOLVING BARRIERS

by Takayuki Sakamoto
of The Pack

3

The Pack, which has been in business for over 40 years, is one of Japan's leading manufacturers of packaging products. We produce and sell cardboard and printed paper products as well as plastic and paper bags. We have three plants total, and I work as a pressman at the paper processing department of the Kanto plant.

In lots of other plants, small group activities take place in QC circles. We call our small groups NC circles, which stands for *Nippon Case*, which was the original name of our company. Anyway, the name isn't as important as the activities that take place in these small groups. The NC circles are places for us to think, talk, and learn together as we tackle the problems we face during the course of our daily work. We share both common goals and the pleasure of achievement.

We start by asking lots of questions about lots of things to decide where to begin kaizen activities. Our inquiries are all related to the following concerns:

- ways to improve operational capabilities
- ways to improve machine performance
- ways to reduce the number of defects
- safety awareness
- 6S activities: organization, tidiness, purity, cleanliness, discipline, commitment

After we isolate a problem we then discuss how to tackle it—how to get from the present situation to the new standard or target. It's a challenging process!

142

I'd like to tell you how we tackled an improvement idea for one of our offset presses. Before our improvement, this press was able to handle stock of varying thickness—as long as the width was between 500mm and 800mm and the length between 750mm and 1100mm.

We had no reason to run larger stock, but we did produce some products that required stock less than 500mm wide and 750mm long. Since our press couldn't accommodate stock smaller than these dimensions, we had to arrange to have some of our work done outside the company.

Offset
Printing Press

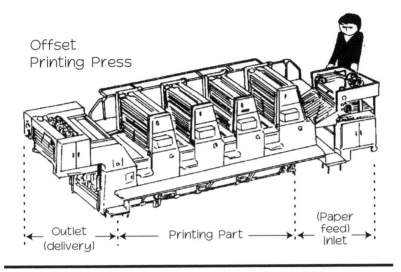

Outlet
(delivery) ← → Printing Part ← → (Paper feed)
Inlet

Current and Desired Capabilities

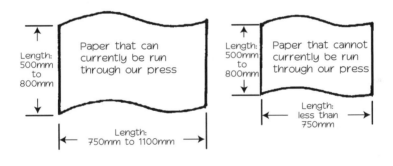

Length:
500mm
to
800mm

Paper that can currently be run through our press

Length:
750mm to 1100mm

Length:
500mm
to
800mm

Paper that cannot currently be run through our press

Length:
less than
750mm

I wondered if it were somehow possible to run smaller stock on our press, and I talked it over with a couple of my colleagues.

"Impossible," one of them said, "the machine specifications simply won't allow it."

"Even if we could do it," the other said, "it'll just mean that our work load will get bigger, and then we'll all suffer."

"But if we can do it," I persisted, "then productivity will increase and we'll have more control over quality and delivery. Plus, I think it will help increase our sales."

We eventually decided that we should set a target of reducing the minimum stock dimensions from 750mm x 500mm to 630mm x 350mm; and also that we should tackle the task within our NC circle.

Within the NC circle, we isolated the following problems:

- At the feed end of the press, the size of the rolling axle prevented the use of stock smaller than 500mm wide.
- At the printing section of the press, the existing patterns would not transfer correctly to the smaller stock.
- Smaller stock didn't fit properly on the outlet mechanism.

Within the group we held a series of discussions meant to find solutions to the problems we had encountered. We tackled them one by one with good results—until we got to the outlet part.

The problem was that the delivery tray couldn't be set for dimensions less than 750mm x 500mm, due to the limitations of the guide rails. My breakthrough came one day when I went to the barber. While waiting my turn I observed a little boy getting his hair cut. The chair was set at its maximum height, but in order to elevate him even higher, the barber had also fitted a

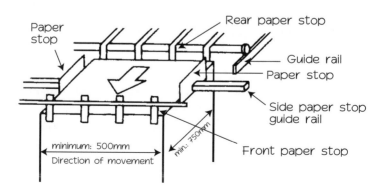

Paper stop

Rear paper stop

Paper stop

Guide rail
Paper stop

Side paper stop guide rail

minimum: 500mm
Direction of movement

min.: 750mm

Front paper stop

special booster seat to the chair. "Why not create a jig?" I asked myself, "to build up the rear paper stop?"

Our step-by-step method of tackling problems led to a big improvement: Our productivity went up, and we were able to achieve higher levels of quality and on-time delivery. On a personal level, I'm proud that we were able to find a solution without turning to the manufacturer of the printing press. I've gained confidence in my abilities, and I feel very strongly now that my job is *not* my job—my job is doing kaizen.

ELIMINATING THE SMALL MISTAKES THAT CAUSE BIG PROBLEMS FOR THE SUBSEQUENT PROCESS

by Kanmi Ishiguro
of Nissan Motors

4

I work in the Kurihama annex of Nissan's Yokohama plant with about 500 other people. We mainly handle machining of parts for engines as well as engine assembly, and I'm in charge of the subassembly process that supplies parts to the engine assembly line. My group was participating reluctantly in kaizen activities in 1985 and 1986, mostly because my supervisor was hounding us to submit ideas.

I knew we couldn't go on like this, so I called a meeting of my group. Together, we identified ten ways to increase morale and boost the amount of kaizen activity:

1. Implement small improvements in the immediate work area.
2. Look for new ways to make work easier.
3. Apply good ideas from other sections to our work.
4. Supervisors and senior employees should lead the way.

5. Be aware of results achieved in other workplaces.
6. Create display charts to make results visible.
7. Make a memo as soon as you notice something.
8. Less experienced employees should look to more experienced workers for inspiration.
9. Consult someone whenever you run into a brick wall.
10. Use part of the award money to socialize and build rapport within the group.

STRATEGY FOR BOOSTING THE QUALITY RATING

Now let me tell you the story *behind* the story. We were having so many problems with our subassembly processes that we

were messing up the subsequent processes right and left. It was awful! I wanted to crawl into a hole when I found out at a plant-wide quality meeting that our process was rated the worst. And this was true month after month.

"I can't take this anymore," I told my group. "I've had enough of being insulted and embarrassed and humiliated. Don't you feel the same?" I asked them to help me restore our reputation.

Reviewing the Current Situation

We began by reviewing our current situation. There were a great many parts to keep track of, and we were relying too much on the memory of operators to make sure that the right part was used in a specific subassembly. Making matters worse was the fact that the racks used to store parts were a mixed-up mess; and also, that our automatic delivery device was not operating correctly.

Accordingly, we decided that opportunities for improvement lay in the following three areas:

1. identifying ways to save time and effort
   • by reducing number of movements
   • by reducing transport distance
   • by working together and communicating better
   • by asking continuously how we might make our work easier
2. finding a way to supplement memory and help operators consistently identify the correct parts
3. determining why the automatic delivery device was malfunctioning and then fixing it

Devising Countermeasures

After identifying the problems and opportunities for improvement, we came up with four countermeasures to address them.

149

Countermeasure 1

The first countermeasure focused on organizing parts and identifying the root causes of the many small problems that were contributing to our larger difficulties. First, I asked that some of our more experienced employees take responsibility for sorting parts and organizing the racks that held them. Second, I asked that other employees take responsibility for isolating root causes of other problems among jobs that they knew best.

Countermeasure 2

After sorting and organizing the parts, we determined which ones were used most frequently and placed them in a central location. This reduced unnecessary movement a great deal.

Countermeasure 3

The third countermeasure was designed to make it possible for anyone, regardless of their experience, to match the right part

Labels above the storage shelves now make it easy for anyone, regardless of their experience, to match the right part to the right subassembly process.

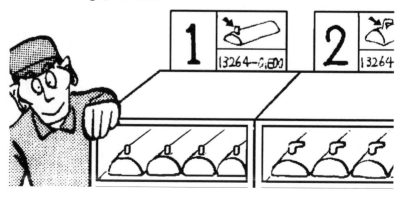

A card rack inspired by the idea of a pigeonhole now ensures that Ishiguro's section supplies its internal customers with the right parts.

to the right subassembly process. Above the storage shelf for each part we placed a label that indicated the part's number as well as its defining characteristics.

As a second part of this countermeasure, I also worked out a system for color-coded address cards to make sure that we always supplied our internal customers, the engine assemblers, with the correct parts. Inspired by the idea of a pigeonhole, I even made a card rack to keep track of the cards.

Countermeasure 4

The remaining challenge, of course, was to fix the problem with the automatic delivery device, but this was beyond our capability. We couldn't isolate the root cause of the problem, because it was actually occurring somewhere other than in our work area. But with help from other departments, such as engineering and maintenance, we were able to reduce significantly the number of problems with the delivery device as well as other important pieces of equipment.

RESULTS OF KAIZEN ACTIVITIES

As a result of our kaizen activities, we dramatically decreased our number of defects and increased the number of improvement ideas to 150 per person per month—among the highest in our plant. Through our efforts we were able to

- reduce the number of stages in the transport of parts
- reduce instances of equipment failure
- standardize work
- improve awareness of quality
- create a bond between night and day shifts
- train new employees more quickly
- build a better relationship with other departments

Personal and Group Transformation

The desire to make lasting improvements motivated me to become thoroughly familiar with the work of my department. In doing so, I could commit myself confidently to a course of action, and this was something the group took to heart. We possess a real team spirit now. No one feels coerced to participate in kaizen activities. We have made a shift from doing just what we're told to being more thoughtful about our own work processes. Furthermore, we possess the shared feeling that there is no problem we can't solve if we work on it together.

Summary of Data

As you can see from the graphs below, we have high levels of participation in kaizen activities, both at the group level and the individual level. From April 1988 through July of that year we focused simply on tackling the problems that had earned us the worst quality record in our plant. From August until October we also concerned ourselves with safety; from October through December we focused on equipment improvement; and then for the remainder of the year we focused on quality. We carried this focus into the first month of the next year before turning to ways that we might conserve energy.

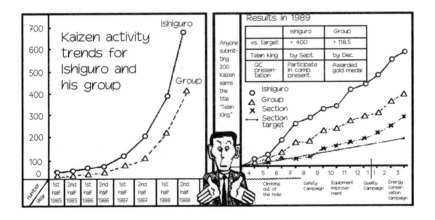

You'll notice that my group continuously increased its improvement activities, moving further from the section target with each passing month. At Nissan, anyone submitting 200 implemented kaizen ideas earns the title *Teian King*. I earned this title in September of 1988, while the group as a whole earned the title a few months later. You'll notice also that in addition to a stable increase in group kaizen activity, every individual in my group performed at a high level.

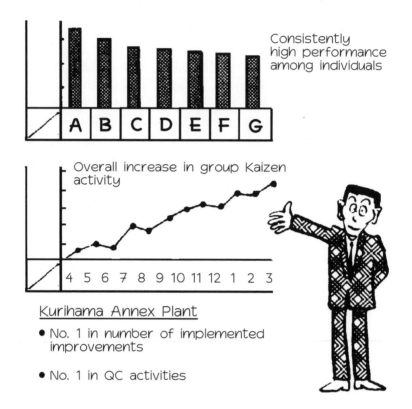

Consistently
high performance
among individuals

A B C D E F G

Overall increase in group Kaizen
activity

4 5 6 7 8 9 10 11 12 1 2 3

Kurihama Annex Plant

- No. 1 in number of implemented
  improvements

- No. 1 in QC activities

154

Thanks to our efforts, the Kurihama annex plant was ranked first among Nissan plants in both the number of improvement ideas and in QC activities. In fact, my group was awarded the gold medal for quality in 1988, and I myself was asked to participate in the company's quality presentation.

I am also proud to report that the idea I created for color-coded address cards has been adopted in other plants. I will keep on trying to improve my work. Possibilities for kaizen are unlimited, because there's frequently a gap between the way things are and the way they should or could be.

KAIZEN IS OUR BIG EVENT

by Yoshikazu Goto
of Mizuno

5

As a member of Mizuno's public relations and advertising department, I help to promote and sell our products. For 81 years, Mizuno has been dedicated not only to developing and selling high-quality sporting goods, but also to promoting sports in general. Some of Japan's most well-respected sports figures, such as golfers Ayako Okamoto and Tsuneyuki Nakajima, and in baseball, the great Ochiai of the Hanshin Tigers, endorse our products. So does the American track star Carl Lewis.

I got involved in promoting kaizen activities in our company by default. Before I immersed myself in kaizen promotion, I was sort of a second-string player. I took on responsibilities that were not clearly assigned to any particular person. I guess you could say I'm sort of a late bloomer. At Mizuno, our improvement efforts focus a great deal on quality, and in January 1985, I was somehow nominated as a TQC promotion leader. Imagine: I had hardly implemented any improvements!

Obviously, this concerned me, but I figured that it was a barrier I needed to break through. Besides, I was of the right age to start assuming more responsibility.

But when I attended my first training seminar as a freshman leader, I was overwhelmed. It seemed that the gap between other leaders and myself was immense. To my credit, however, I am naturally competitive. After some soul searching, I decided that I would become number one in promoting kaizen activities at Mizuno.

In the previous year, 1984, Mizuno had paid over 30 upper-grade rewards for implemented improvements. Based on this figure, I set a target for the advertising department of three implemented improvements per person per month. People were not pleased. I understood why. In 1984, our department had only had an average of .9 implemented improvements per person per month. Therefore, I was asking for three times their previous effort of 10.8 improvements per person per year. Because this is an average, it of course meant that some people had submitted a lot of ideas while others had submitted none. In fact, I discovered that most people had not submitted any improvements.

FIVE STRATEGIES FOR REACHING THE TARGET

You have to understand that my colleagues are an individualistic bunch with unyielding spirits. Trying to force them to participate simply would not work. I had to find ways to appeal to their individuality.

1. Appeal to Their Creative Pride

All people are creative in different ways, but advertising people in particular define themselves in terms of creativity. I communicated the following message: How creative is it to continue doing the same things time after time and day after day? I suggested that if they were truly creative, everyone should be able to think of an improvement and implement it at least once a week.

2. Appeal to Their Competitive Spirit and Sense of Fun

Since the advertising department is accustomed to working in groups and most of them like events, I guessed correctly that they would enjoy competing against one another in groups. I drew a pie chart for each of the groups. I divided each pie into pieces, and every time someone in a group implemented an improvement, I filled in a piece of their pie. The object, of course, was to fill in an entire pie. The groups were able to see quickly and easily how they were doing relative to their competitors.

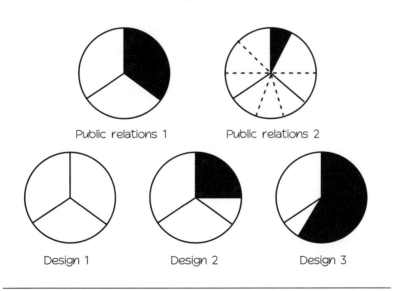

Public relations 1   Public relations 2

Design 1   Design 2   Design 3

3. Display and Use Data Wisely

Even if I was very busy, if someone brought me a kaizen report, I updated the appropriate pie chart immediately. And I encouraged people as I did it. "Gee," I would say, "you are very quick this month. One more improvement and you'll have colored in the whole pie."

Just by doing these three things, the number of implemented improvements per person in our department skyrocketed to ten per month. In fact, our department, which consists of only 18 people, beat out a department with nearly 100 people in it for the most implemented improvements. As you can imagine, I was very pleased.

From the data I'd accumulated, I created more charts, tracking trends not only by group, but also by age and sex. I was concerned about some of the findings. Although overall participation was high, I discovered that participation by men and women over the age of 40 was much lower than participation of those in their 20s and 30s. In addition, participation among women of all ages was very low.

Rather than keeping this data to myself, I made it available for display. I had hoped that doing so would motivate those in their 40s to greater levels of participation. After all, these are the people to whom the younger employees are supposed to look for guidance. Therefore, employees over 40 might lose face if they failed to boost their participation levels. Levels among older men did increase, but to my chagrin, participation by women did not improve.

4. Involve Managers

There are two important ways in which managers may favorably influence participation in improvement activities. The first is when they hold themselves accountable for reaching the same target expected of their subordinates. The manager of the advertising department, for example, was responsible for implementing three improvements per month, just like the rest of us.

Second, it adds value to rewards when managers hand them out. The director of our department, for instance, holds a meeting with employees every month. During this meeting he reviews the improvements that have been implemented and personally rewards people for their efforts.

5. Clarify and Publicize Results

In order to keep department members' morale high, I asked TQC headquarters to publish our kaizen statistics in the monthly *TQC News*. We were consistently included among a list of the top ten kaizen producing departments in the company. Here are some other important results that I shared: 11 percent of the people in the advertising department received upper-grade rewards; the number of upper-grade rewards in the company in general increased from 30 the previous year to 40 in 1985! In addition, The advertising department led the company in the number of implemented improvements for two years in a row.

CONCLUDING REMARKS

I'm also proud to report that I have become quite a good submitter myself. Before becoming a leader, I used to submit no more than five kaizen per year. But for the last two years, I have submitted 50. Let me tell you about one simple improvement I made recently.

In the advertising department, we use video cameras fairly regularly. There are 14 irregularly placed pins on the cable, and these pins need to be plugged into 14 corresponding holes on the camera.

By trial and error, people were eventually able to fit the plug to the camera socket. Unfortunately, we sometimes damaged pins in the process. To prevent this problem from recurring, I found arrow stickers that I attached both to the plug and the terminal. Now, anyone can connect the cable to the camera on the first try just by joining the arrows. (See drawing on page 160.)

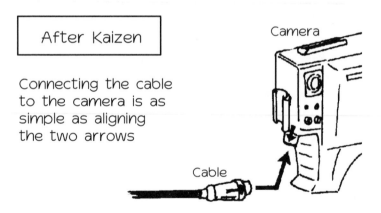

I've gotten into the habit of jotting ideas down as they come to me. I even keep memo pads in the bathroom at home, as well as on the nightstand by my bed.

In January of 1987, I handed over the responsibility for kaizen promotion to another leader. The only thing I was not able to accomplish during my tenure was boosting the participation among women in our department. This new fellow has managed to succeed where I failed, however. I'm not sure how he's done it. I suspect he may be more naturally charming than I.

CONCEPTUAL

KAIZEN

by Emiko Kondo
of Meiji Dairy Products

6

There are two types of kaizen: job kaizen and conceptual kaizen. Job kaizen involves the things people do to make their work easier and more efficient. Conceptual kaizen has more to do with products. During the course of my work in the sales office of Meiji Dairy Products, I have come to specialize in conceptual kaizen.

I joined the company in 1982, and although managers talked about the kaizen system, I really wasn't very interested. You can imagine how I felt, when two years later, my supervisor appointed me a kaizen promotion committee member. This caused me a great deal of anxiety. But that's all behind me now.

At about the time I was appointed part of the promotion committee, the company began making an earnest attempt to boost participation. People started to become more enthusiastic about the kaizen system. I was no exception. All my ideas were related to our products, though, rather than to my work specifically.

IDEAS COME FROM EVERYDAY LIFE

From where did my ideas come? Ideas never come just from sitting in front of a kaizen sheet; they come from experience—from everyday life.

At the time, I really enjoyed cooking a lot, and after work, I used to drive to the supermarket to pick up ingredients for that night's dinner. What was really interesting was that once I became aware of kaizen, it changed the way I shopped. Before becoming aware of kaizen, I was strictly interested in comparing prices and freshness. After becoming aware of kaizen, however, I took a greater interest in the variety of products themselves. I compared our products to our competitors', looked to non-competing products for ideas that we might apply to our products, and noticed trends in packaging as well as new product introductions. Not only did I become more conscious of products, but I also listened carefully to what customers were saying.

I realized that when you start looking at things differently there are lots of sources for kaizen: television, magazines, and even casual conversations with family and friends. As my ideas were adopted, I changed my point of view toward the company as well. Before, I had a very narrow view of my own role in the company. But then I became familiar with other products we made, and this widened my horizons. Feedback from my supervisor also made me more aware of things such as costs and technical issues.

I would give the following advice to people who are trying to generate ideas:

- Give your imagination free rein. This is no time to think conservatively!
- Don't be pretentious.
- Create reasonable goals for yourself.
- Write down ideas as soon as they come to you; have a memo pad handy at all times.

• Keep your kaizen sheets as simple as possible, using tables and drawings as much as possible to illustrate your ideas.

I've been quite imaginative with some of my ideas, if I do say so myself—maybe too imaginative. In the past I've come up with new ideas for food products, and some of them have been pretty outrageous! How does a yogurt and mashed potato croquette sound? Or fruit-yogurt porridge? These were two of my more spectacular failures. Of course, they never got beyond the idea stage. I wouldn't want to eat these things myself, so I couldn't imagine that our customers would want to eat them either.

REVERSE ICE CREAM SANDWICHES

Although I've had some pretty outrageous ideas for new products, I've also had some ideas that were adopted. The idea for reverse ice cream sandwiches came to me one day when I was in the freezer section of my local supermarket. There I overheard a conversation between a mother and her child. The child was throwing a tantrum because the mother would not buy him an ice

Three Variations on the Reverse
Ice Cream Sandwich Idea

Cookie soaked in milk or liquer

Thin slice of sponge cake soaked in syrup

Ice cream

Chocolate ice cream

Chocolate coating

Wafer

Vanilla ice cream

Ice cream

cream sandwich. "No," the woman said, "it's crumbly and will make a big mess."

"How about turning the ice cream sandwich inside out?" I thought. The illustration shows three different variations of this idea that were adopted.

THE MOO-MOO CLIP CAMPAIGN

When we have visitors at our office, we offer them fruit juice or milk instead of coffee. This used to create a problem. Open cartons of milk in the refrigerator sometimes got knocked over and spilled, making a big mess. Also, open dairy products tend to absorb the smells of other foods. We needed a way to keep milk fresh and also keep it from spilling.

We tried taping the cartons closed or using a variety of different binder clips. These methods were effective, but they looked so tacky! That's how I thought of the idea for a little plastic clip in the shape of a cow. Obviously, this is not something designed for adults. But kids love them, and they urge parents to buy them. Since the clips are so inexpensive, this is no problem.

OOPS

SPLAT !

Opened dairy products may spill, and they quickly absorb smells from other foods in the refrigerator

Kids love the moo-moo clip because it's cute. Adults will buy it because it's inexpensive, it's durable, and it works.

Customer comments

I need it

I must have it

cute!

I want it

NEW PACKAGING FOR SHREDDED CHEESE

Sometimes I like to make pizza at home, using shredded mozzarella cheese made by Meiji Dairy Products, of course! But it

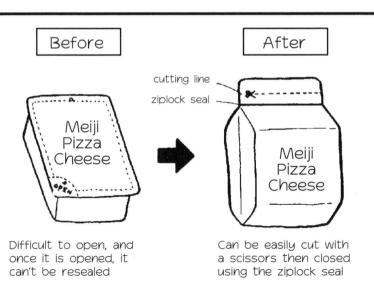

Before

After

cutting line

ziplock seal

Meiji Pizza Cheese

Meiji Pizza Cheese

Difficult to open, and once it is opened, it can't be resealed

Can be easily cut with a scissors then closed using the ziplock seal

always used to bother me that there was no way of resealing the package, which made it likely that the leftover cheese would get dried out and become tasteless. Our competitors also packaged the cheese in a way that did not allow for resealing. The drawing shows my improvement idea, which won an award from corporate headquarters and was adopted companywide for packaging all our cheeses.

LET YOUR CURIOSITY GUIDE YOU

Curiosity is a great asset when it comes to kaizen. The more curious you get about things, the more information you absorb, which makes it easy to come up with ideas. When you submit one kaizen, it increases your awareness of other problems, which leads you to the next improvement. By continuing to let my curiosity guide me, I look forward to coming up with many more ideas that we can use to produce tasty, convenient, and even amusing products.

POSTSCRIPT

The contents of this book are based on tried
and true training techniques of the Japan Human
Relations Association. We've tried to distill from
our presentations, seminars, and study groups the most
important aspects of introducing, developing, and sustaining
kaizen activities.

The beauty of participating in kaizen teian training events is
that companies almost always see a return on their investment
quite quickly. Kaizen reporting generates documentation that
shows the number of improvements implemented, levels of participation, and rewards. Improvement is measurable, and the
numbers are hard to fudge. Therefore, representatives from the
companies we train take their roles seriously, both during and
after the training events.

As a result, we have been fortunate to have a steady source
of feedback. Examination of daily improvement activities at
various companies, as well as earnest discussions and even

arguments, has helped to refine our understanding of the improvement process.

Most of the discussions and arguments have taken place with a number of "kaizen crazy" individuals we've met over the years. Every company has such people. They are a bit stubborn, but they believe passionately that every employee is capable of making creative improvements to his or her work. These improvement enthusiasts, therefore, are real champions of employee development. They are not intimidated by obstacles, and they don't hesitate to smash the status quo of existing systems and management methods. This book is a result of the support and improvements made by these people, and we'd like to express our deep gratitude to them for their dedication and perseverance.

Finally, we'd like to end by reminding you that once ideas such as those in this book get into print, they start to become antiquated. We can perhaps never really capture the essence of kaizen in a book, because management techniques continuously change and develop. Nevertheless, we sincerely hope that this three-volume series provides a strong foundation from which to develop more efficient and effective bottom-up methods of improvement.

INDEX

BOOKS FROM PRODUCTIVITY PRESS

Productivity Press publishes and distributes materials on continuous improvement in productivity, quality, and the creative involvement of all employees. Many of our products are direct source materials from Japan that have been translated into English for the first time and are available exclusively from Productivity. Supplemental products and services include membership groups, conferences, seminars, in-house training and consulting, audio-visual training programs, and industrial study missions.

Call toll-free 1-800-394-6868 for our free catalog.

Secrets of a Successful Employee Recognition System
Daniel C. Boyle

As the human resource manager of a failing manufacturing plant, Dan Boyle was desperate to find a way to motivate employees and break down the barrier between management and the union. He came up with a simple idea—say thank you to you employees for doing their job. In *Secrets of a Successful Employee Recognition System*, Boyle outlines how to begin and run a 100 Club program. Filled with case studies and detailed guidelines, this book underscores the power behind thanking your employees for a job well done.
ISBN 1-56327-083-8 / 250 pages / $25.00 / Order SECRET-B250

40 Years, 20 Million Ideas
The Toyota Suggestion System
Yuzo Yasuda

This fascinating book describes how Toyota generated tremendous employee involvement in their creative idea suggestion system. It reviews the program's origins, Toyota's internal promotion of the system, and examples of actual suggestions and how they were used. Personal accounts and anecdotes flavor the text and address problems encountered and their resolutions.
ISBN 0-915299-74-7 / 208 pages / $39.95 / Order 4020-B250

Productivity Press, Inc. Dept. BK, P.O. Box 13390, Portland, OR 97213-0390
Telephone: 1-800-394-6868   Fax: 1-800-394-6286

The Benchmarking Management Guide
American Productivity & Quality Center

If you're planning, organizing, or actually undertaking a benchmarking program, you need the most authoritative source of information to help you get started and to manage the process all the way through. Written expressly for managers of benchmarking projects by the APQC's renowned International Benchmarking Clearinghouse, this guide provides exclusive information from members who have already paved the way. It includes information on training courses and ways to apply Baldrige, Deming, and ISO 9000 criteria for internal assessment, and has a complete bibliography of benchmarking literature.
ISBN 1-56327-045-5 / 260 pages / $39.95 / Order BMG-B250

Feedback Toolkit
16 Tools for Better Communication in the Workplace
Rick Maurer

In companies striving to reduce hierarchy and foster trust and responsible participation, good person-to-person feedback can be as important as sophisticated computer technology in enabling effective teamwork. Feedback is an important map of your situation, a way to tell whether you are "on or off track." Used well, feedback can motivate people to their highest level of performance. Despite its significance, this level of information sharing makes most managers uncomfortable. Feedback Toolkit addresses this natural hesitation with an easy-to-grasp 6-step framework and 16 practical and creative approaches for giving and receiving feedback with individuals and groups. Maurer's reality-tested methods in *Feedback Toolkit* are indispensable equipment for managers and teams in every organization.
ISBN 1-56327-056-0 / 109 pages / $15.00 / Order FEED-B250

Caught in the Middle
A Leadership Guide for Partnership in the Workplace
Rick Maurer

Managers today are caught between old skills and new expectations. You're expected not only to improve quality and services, but also to get staff more involved. This stimulating book provides the inspiration and know-how to achieve these goals as it brings to light the rewards of establishing a real partnership with your staff. Includes self-assessment questionnaires.
ISBN 1-56327-004-8 / 258 pages / $29.95 / Order CAUGHT-B250

Productivity Press, Inc. Dept. BK, P.O. Box 13390, Portland, OR 97213-0390
Telephone: 1-800-394-6868   Fax: 1-800-394-6286

CEDAC
A Tool for Continuous Systematic Improvement
Ryuji Fukuda

CEDAC® encompasses three tools for continuous systematic improvement: window analysis (for identifying problems), the CEDAC diagram (a modification of the classic "fishbone diagram," for analyzing problems and developing standards), and window development (for ensuring adherence to standards). This manual provides directions for setting up and using CEDAC. Sample forms included.
ISBN 0-915299-26-7 / 144 pages / $55.00 / Order CEDAC-B250

Fast Focus on TQM
A Concise Guide to Companywide Learning
Derm Barrett

Finally, here's one source for all your TQM questions. Compiled in this concise, easy-to-read handbook are definitions and detailed explanations of over 160 key terms used in TQM. Organized in a simple alphabetical glossary form, the book can be used either as a primer for anyone being introduced to TQM or as a complete reference guide. It helps to align teams, departments, or entire organizations in a common understanding and use of TQM terminology. For anyone entering or currently involved in TQM, this is one resource you must have.
ISBN 1-56327-049-8 / 186 pages / $19.95 / Order FAST-B250

Handbook for Personal Productivity
Henry E. Liebling

A little book with a lot of power that will help you become more successful and satisfied at work, as well as in your personal life. This pocket-sized handbook offers sections on personal productivity improvement, team achievement, quality customer service, improving your health, and how to get the most out of workshops and seminars. Special bulk discounts are available (call for more information).
ISBN 0-915299-94-1 / 128 pages / $9.00 paper / Order PP-B250

Productivity Press, Inc. Dept. BK, P.O. Box 13390, Portland, OR 97213-0390
Telephone: 1-800-394-6868   Fax: 1-800-394-6286

Handbook for Productivity Measurement and Improvement
William F. Christopher and Carl G. Thor, eds.

An unparalleled resource! In over 100 chapters, nearly 80 front-runners in the quality movement reveal the evolving theory and specific practices of world-class organizations. Spanning a wide variety of industries and business sectors, they discuss quality and productivity in manufacturing, service industries, profit centers, administration, nonprofit and government institutions, health care and education. Contributors include Robert C. Camp, Peter F. Drucker, Jay W. Forrester, Joseph M. Juran, Robert S. Kaplan, John W. Kendrick, Yasuhiro Monden, and Lester C. Thurow. Comprehensive in scope and organized for easy reference, this compendium belongs in every company and academic institution concerned with business and industrial viability.
ISBN 1-56327-007-2 / 1344 pages / $90.00 / Order HPM-B250

The Hunters and the Hunted
A Non-Linear Solution for American Industry
James B. Swartz

Because our competitive environment changes so rapidly—weekly, even daily—if you want to survive, you have to stay on top of those changes. Otherwise, you become prey to your competitors. Hunters continuously change and learn; anyone who doesn't becomes the hunted and sooner or later will be devoured. This unusual non-fiction novel provides a veritable crash course in continuous transformation. It offers lessons from real-life companies and introduces many industrial gurus as characters, as well providing a riveting story of two strong people struggling to turn their company around. *The Hunters and the Hunted* doesn't simply tell you how to change; it puts you inside the change process itself.
ISBN 1-56327-043-9 / 582 pages / $45.00 / Order HUNT-B250

Productivity Press, Inc. Dept. BK, P.O. Box 13390, Portland, OR 97213-0390
Telephone: 1-800-394-6868   Fax: 1-800-394-6286

The Idea Book
Improvement Through TEI (Total Employee Involvement)
Japan Human Relations Association

At last, a book showing how to create Total Employee Involvement (TEI) and get hundreds of ideas from each employee every year to improve every aspect of your organization. Gathering improvement ideas from your entire workforce is a must for global competitiveness. *The Idea Book*, heavily illustrated, is a hands-on teaching tool for workers and supervisors to refer to again and again. Perfect for study groups, too.
ISBN 0-915299-22-4 / 232 pages / $55.00 / Order IDEA-B250

Individual Motivation
Removing the Blocks to Creative Involvement
Etienne Minarik

The key to gaining the competitive advantage in a saturated market is to use existing resources more efficiently and creatively. This book shows managers how to turn employees' "negative individualism" into creativity and initiative. It describes the shift in corporate culture necessary to enable front-line employees to use their knowledge about product and process to the company's greatest benefit.
ISBN 0-915299-85-2 / 263 pages / $29.95 / Order INDM-B250

Kaizen Teian 1
Developing Systems for Continuous Improvement Through Employee Suggestions
Japan Human Relations Association (ed.)

Especially relevant for middle and upper managers, this book focuses on the role of managers as catalysts in spurring employee ideas and facilitating their implementation. It explains how to run a proposal program on a day-to-day basis and outlines the policies that support a "bottom-up" system of innovation and defines the three main objectives of *kaizen teian*: to build participation, develop individual skills, and achieve higher profits.
ISBN 0-915299-89-5 / 217 pages / $39.95 / Order KT1-B250

Productivity Press, Inc. Dept. BK, P.O. Box 13390, Portland, OR 97213-0390
Telephone: 1-800-394-6868   Fax: 1-800-394-6286

Kaizen Teian 2
Guiding Continuous Improvement Through Employee Suggestions
Japan Human Relations Association (ed.)

Building on the concepts covered in *Kaizen Teian I*, this second volume examines in depth how to implement kaizen teian—a continuous improvement suggestions system. Managers will learn techniques for getting employees to think creatively about workplace improvements and how to run a successful proposal program.
ISBN 0-915299-53-4 / 221 pages / $40.00 / Order KT2-B250

Managerial Engineering
Techniques for Improving Quality and Productivity in the Workplace
Ryuji Fukuda

A proven path to managerial success, based on reliable methods developed by one of Japan's leading productivity experts and winner of the coveted Deming Prize for quality. Dr. W. Edwards Deming, world-famous consultant on quality, said that the book "provides an excellent and clear description of the devotion and methods of Japanese management to continual improvement of quality." (Training programs on CEDAC, the award-winning system outlined in this book, are also available from Productivity.)
ISBN 0-915299-09-7 / 208 pages / $44.95 / Order ME-B250

Measuring, Managing, and Maximizing Performance
Will Kaydos

You do not need to be an exceptionally skilled technician or inspirational leader to improve your company's quality and productivity. In non-technical, jargon-free, practical terms this book details the entire process of improving performance, from why and how the improvement process work to what must be done to begin and to sustain continuous improvement of performance. Special emphasis is given to the role that performance measurement plays in identifying problems and opportunities.
ISBN 0-915299-98-4 / 284 pages / $39.95 / Order MMMP-B250

Productivity Press, Inc. Dept. BK, P.O. Box 13390, Portland, OR 97213-0390
Telephone: 1-800-394-6868   Fax: 1-800-394-6286

A New American TQM
Four Practical Revolutions in Management
Shoji Shiba, Alan Graham, and David Walden

For TQM to succeed in America, you need to create an American-style "learning organization" with the full commitment and understanding of senior managers and executives. Written expressly for this audience, *A New American TQM* offers a comprehensive and detailed explanation of TQM and how to implement it, based on courses taught at MIT's Sloan School of Management and the Center for Quality Management, a consortium of American companies. Full of case studies and amply illustrated, the book examines major quality tools and how they are being used by the most progressive American companies today.
ISBN 1-56327-032-3 / 606 pages / $49.95 / Order NATQM-B250

The Service Industry Idea Book
Employee Involvement in Retail and Office Improvement
Japan Human Relations Association (ed.)

This book presents an improvement proposal system designed especially for customer service and administrative employees. Initial chapters about why suggestions are important and how to write persuasive improvement proposals are followed by two chapters of illustrated examples and case histories from various services industries and office and administrative situations.
ISBN 0-915299-65-8 / 294 pages / $49.95 / Order SIDEA-B250

The Teamwork Advantage
An Inside Look at Japanese Product and Technology Development
Jeffrey L. Funk

How are so many Japanese manufacturing firms shortening product time-to-market, reducing costs, and improving quality? The answer is teamwork. Dr. Funk spent 18 months as a visiting engineer at Mitsubishi and Yokogawa Hokushin Electric and knows firsthand how Japanese corporate culture promotes effective teamwork in production, design, and technology development. Here's a penetrating case study and analysis that presents a truly viable model for the West.
ISBN 0-915299-69-0 / 508 pages / $49.95 / Order TEAMAD-B250

Productivity Press, Inc. Dept. BK, P.O. Box 13390, Portland, OR 97213-0390
Telephone: 1-800-394-6868   Fax: 1-800-394-6286

The Unshackled Organization
Facing the Challenge of Unpredictability Through Spontaneous Reorganization
Jeffrey Goldstein

Managers should not necessarily try to solve all the internal problems within their organizations; intervention may help in the short term, but in the long run may inhibit true problem-solving change from taking place. And change is the real goal. Through change comes real hope for improvement. Goldstein explores how change happens within an organization using some of the most leading-edge scientific and social theories about change and reveals that only through "self-organization" can natural, lasting change occur. This book is a pragmatic guide for managers, executives, consultants, and other change agents.
ISBN 1-56327-048-X / 208 pages / $25.00 / Order UO-B250

The Visual Factory
Building Participation Through Shared Information
Michel Greif

If you're aware of the tremendous improvements achieved in productivity and quality as a result of employee involvement, then you'll appreciate the great value of creating a visual factory. This book shows how visual management can make the factory a place where workers and supervisors freely communicate and take improvement action. It details how to develop meeting and communication areas, communicate work standards and instructions, use visual production controls such as kanban, and make goals and progress visible. Includes more than 200 diagrams and photos.
ISBN 0-915299-67-4 / 305 pages / $55.00 / Order VFAC-B250

Productivity Press, Inc. Dept. BK, P.O. Box 13390, Portland, OR 97213-0390
Telephone: 1-800-394-6868   Fax: 1-800-394-6286

TO ORDER: Write, phone, or fax Productivity Press, Dept. BK, P.O. Box 13390, Portland, OR 97213-0390, phone 1-800-394-6868, fax 1-800-394-6286. Send check or charge to your credit card (American Express, Visa, MasterCard accepted).

U.S. ORDERS: Add $5 shipping for first book, $2 each additional for UPS surface delivery. We offer attractive quantity discounts for bulk purchases of individual titles; call for more information.

INTERNATIONAL ORDERS: Write, phone, or fax for quote and indicate shipping method desired. For international callers, telephone number is 503-235-0600 and fax number is 503-235-0909. Prepayment in U.S. dollars must accompany your order (checks must be drawn on U.S. banks). When quote is returned with payment, your order will be shipped promptly by the method requested.

NOTE: Prices are in U.S. dollars and are subject to change without notice.

Productivity Press, Inc. Dept. BK, P.O. Box 13390, Portland, OR 97213-0390
Telephone: 1-800-394-6868   Fax: 1-800-394-6286